SOUNDS CLEAR
- TARGETING ENGLISH PRONUNCIATION -

음원파일 다운로드 안내

- 한국문화사 자료실 (http://hph.co.kr) 접속 → 자료실 → sounds clear 폴더 → 음원파일 다운로드

- 유튜브에 '도서출판 한국문화사'를 검색하세요.

SOUNDS CLEAR

제2판

Targeting English Pronunciation

박미애 · Claudia Tumba 지음

한국문화사

SOUNDS CLEAR
TARGETING ENGLISH PRONUNCIATION

1판 1쇄 발행 2020년 7월 31일
2판 1쇄 발행 2023년 2월 28일

지 은 이 ｜ 박미애·Claudia Tumba
펴 낸 이 ｜ 김진수
펴 낸 곳 ｜ 한국문화사
등   록 ｜ 제1994-9호
주   소 ｜ 서울특별시 성동구 아차산로49, 404호(성수동1가, 서울숲코오롱디지털타워3차)
전   화 ｜ 02-464-7708
팩   스 ｜ 02-499-0846
이 메 일 ｜ hkm7708@daum.net
홈페이지 ｜ http://hph.co.kr

ISBN   979-11-6919-094-7 93740

· 잘못된 책은 구매처에서 바꾸어 드립니다.
· 이 책의 내용은 저작권법에 따라 보호받고 있습니다.
· 책값은 뒤표지에 있습니다.

오류를 발견하셨다면 이메일이나 홈페이지를 통해 제보해주세요.
소중한 의견을 모아 더 좋은 책을 만들겠습니다.

Contents

To the Instructor	14
To the Student	17
Guide to the Symbols	19

Chapter 1 SYLLABLES — 23

» **BACKGROUND INFORMATION**	23
» **PRACTICE ACTIVITIES**	26
LISTEN 1	26
LISTEN 2	27
LISTEN 3	27
LISTEN AND SPEAK	28
SPEAK 1: Syllable Maze	28
SPEAK 2: Counting Syllables	29
SPEAK 3: Change the Lyrics	30

Chapter 2 STRESSED AND UNSTRESSED SYLLABLES — 33

PART 1. STRESS — 33

» **BACKGROUND INFORMATION**	33
» **PRACTICE ACTIVITIES**	35
LISTEN 1	35
LISTEN 2	36
LISTEN 3	36

PART 2. UNSTRESS — 37

- **BACKGROUND INFORMATION** — 37
- **PRACTICE ACTIVITIES** — 38
  - LISTEN 1 — 38
  - LISTEN 2 — 38
  - SPEAK 1: Word Stress Bingo — 39
  - SPEAK 2: Highlighting and Weakening Syllables — 40
  - SPEAK 3: Role-Play Situations — 41

Chapter 3 PREDICTABLE WORD STRESS — 43

- **BACKGROUND INFORMATION** — 43

PART 1. STRESS PATTERNS ACCORDING TO SYLLABLE WEIGHT AND WORD CATEGORY — 44

- **PRACTICE ACTIVITIES** — 44
  - LISTEN 1 — 44
  - LISTEN 2 — 45
  - LISTEN 3 — 45
  - SPEAK 1: Airport Check-in — 47
  - SPEAK 2: Have You Ever...? — 48

PART 2. STRESS PATTERNS IN MORPHOLOGICALLY COMPLEX WORDS — 49

- **PRACTICE ACTIVITIES** — 49
  - LISTEN 1 — 49
  - LISTEN 2 — 50
  - LISTEN 3 — 51

LISTEN 4	53
LISTEN 5	54
SPEAK 1: College Life Dice Bingo	55
SPEAK 2: The Perfect Date Survey	56

PART 3. STRESS PATTERNS ACCORDING TO SPELLING — 57

» **PRACTICE ACTIVITIES** — 57

LISTEN 1	57
SPEAK 1: Ty & Teen Snakes and Ladders	58
SPEAK 2: Personality Interview	58

Chapter 4 RHYTHM IN SENTENCES — 61

» **BACKGROUND INFORMATION** — 61

» **PRACTICE ACTIVITIES** — 63

LISTEN 1	63
LISTEN 2	64
LISTEN 3	64
SPEAK 1: Ordering Drinks at a Cafe	65
SPEAK 2: Team Project	67

Chapter 5 PHRASING AND LINKING — 69

» **BACKGROUND INFORMATION** — 69

» **PRACTICE ACTIVITIES** — 71

LISTEN 1	71
LISTEN 2	71

LISTEN 3	72
LISTEN AND SPEAK	73
SPEAK 1: Worst Day Ever?	75
SPEAK 2: Chants & Poems	77
SPEAK 3: One Fry, Two Fries	78

Chapter 6 PROMINENCE IN DISCOURSE   79

» **BACKGROUND INFORMATION**	79
» **PRACTICE ACTIVITIES**	80
LISTEN 1	80
LISTEN 2	81
LISTEN AND SPEAK	82
SPEAK 1: The Danger of a Single Story	83
SPEAK 2: Focus Tic Tac Toe	84
SPEAK 3: Eliciting Vocabulary	85
SPEAK 4: Food Debate	86

Chapter 7 INTONATION   87

» **BACKGROUND INFORMATION**	87
» **PRACTICE ACTIVITIES**	88
LISTEN 1	88
LISTEN 2	89
LISTEN AND SPEAK	91
SPEAK 1: Asking Questions	92
SPEAK 2: Lesson Introduction	93

SPEAK 3: Intonation Bingo	94
SPEAK 4: The Finish Line	94

Chapter 8 CONSONANTS — 95

- » **BACKGROUND INFORMATION** — 95

Voiceless vs. Voiced Consonants in English — 102
- » **PRACTICE ACTIVITIES** — 103
  - LISTEN 1 — 103

/p/ as in *pin* vs. /f/ as in *fin* — 105
- » **PRACTICE ACTIVITIES** — 105
  - LISTEN 1 — 105
  - LISTEN 2 — 105
  - LISTEN AND SPEAK — 106
  - SPEAK 1: Classroom Quiz — 107
  - SPEAK 2: Are You Adulting? — 109

/b/ as in *boat* vs. /v/ as in *vote* — 110
- » **PRACTICE ACTIVITIES** — 110
  - LISTEN 1 — 110
  - LISTEN 2 — 110
  - LISTEN AND SPEAK — 111
  - SPEAK 1: Guess Who — 112
  - SPEAK 2: Giving Directions — 113

/θ/ as in *think* vs. /s/ as in *sink* — 114
» **PRACTICE ACTIVITIES** — 114
- LISTEN 1 — 114
- LISTEN 2 — 114
- LISTEN AND SPEAK — 115
- SPEAK 1: Tongue Twisters — 116
- SPEAK 2: Battleship — 118

/ð/ as in *though* vs. /d/ as in *dough* — 119
» **PRACTICE ACTIVITIES** — 119
- LISTEN 1 — 119
- LISTEN 2 — 119
- LISTEN AND SPEAK — 120
- SPEAK 1: Whose Is It? — 122
- SPEAK 2: Desert Island — 123

/r/ as in *rent* vs. /l/ as in *lent* — 124
» **PRACTICE ACTIVITIES** — 125
- LISTEN 1 — 125
- LISTEN 2 — 125
- LISTEN AND SPEAK — 126
- SPEAK 1: The Dial Pad Game — 127
- SPEAK 2: Lesson Review — 128

/ʒ/ as in *usual* vs. /dʒ/ as in *judge* vs. /z/ as in *zoo* — 129
» **PRACTICE ACTIVITIES** — 130
- LISTEN 1 — 130

LISTEN 2	130
LISTEN AND SPEAK	131
SPEAK 1: Dots and Boxes	132
SPEAK 2: The Time Capsule	133

Chapter 9   VOWELS   135

» **BACKGROUND INFORMATION**   135

/iy/ as in *leap* vs. /ɪ/ as in *lip*   138

» **PRACTICE ACTIVITIES**   139

LISTEN 1	139
LISTEN 2	139
LISTEN AND SPEAK	140
SPEAK 1: Tongue Twisters	141
SPEAK 2: OXO Game	142

/ey/ as in *mate* vs. /ɛ/ as in *met*   143

» **PRACTICE ACTIVITIES**   144

LISTEN 1	144
LISTEN 2	144
LISTEN AND SPEAK	145
SPEAK 1: Find the Objects	146
SPEAK 2: American Slang	147

/æ/ as in *mat* vs. /ɛ/ as in *met*   148

» **PRACTICE ACTIVITIES**   149

LISTEN 1	149

LISTEN 2	149
LISTEN AND SPEAK	150
SPEAK 1: Connect Four	151
SPEAK 2: A Visit to the School Nurse	151

/ʌ/ as in *hut* vs. /ɑ/ as in *hot* — 152

» **PRACTICE ACTIVITIES** — 153

LISTEN 1	153
LISTEN 2	153
LISTEN AND SPEAK	154
SPEAK 1: Family Tree	154
SPEAK 2: Common English Errors	155
SPEAK 3: Pronunciation Pyramid Page	156

/uw/ as in *Luke* vs. /ʊ/ as in *look* — 157

» **PRACTICE ACTIVITIES** — 158

LISTEN 1	158
LISTEN 2	158
LISTEN AND SPEAK	159
SPEAK 1: Blankety Blank – What to Say When…	160
SPEAK 2: Daily Activities	161

/ow/ as in *no* vs. /ɔ/ as in *all* vs. /ʌ/ as in *null* — 162

» **PRACTICE ACTIVITIES** — 163

LISTEN 1	163
LISTEN 2	163
LISTEN AND SPEAK	164

SPEAK 1: Carnival Bingo 165
SPEAK 2: Setting Homework 165

Practice Activity Answer Keys 167
APPENDIX: Activity Worksheet 181

To the Instructor

Sounds Clear introduces English pronunciation to intermediate and advanced English learners, particularly those who speak Korean as a first language. It intends to address students' pronunciation needs, the difficulties students often come across, and ways to improve their English pronunciation. Also, *Sounds Clear* is a useful resource for experienced or trainee English teachers who currently teach or will teach students English in the future. It enables teachers and trainee teachers to easily integrate pronunciation points into their day-to-day teaching. It is an excellent resource as a course textbook or as a comprehensive program for self-study.

The background information provides clear explanations for target pronunciation aspects in each chapter and attempts to promote students' and teachers' knowledge of them. It also helps students understand how the target elements have an influence on pronunciation intelligibility. Moreover, this textbook's adaptable and straightforward activities require little preparation and cover a wide range of topics, making them ideal for use in everyday conversations and when giving teaching demonstrations, micro-teaching, or lesson planning. *Sounds Clear* provides various scenarios both for students to practice useful daily expressions and for teachers to practice classroom phrases and expressions. These expressions are essential for establishing a suitable environment of communication. Such an environment is especially crucial for learners whose sole social context for practicing English will be your class.

Pronunciation is an integral part of the oral language skills of listening and speaking. Although for some English students and teachers native-like English pronunciation is a desirable goal to attain, intelligibility, however, is more widely accepted as a reasonable and realistic goal for a majority of English teachers and students, with a focus of language as a system of exchanging meanings for communication, as well as a system of rules. *Sounds Clear* places focus on both segmental and suprasegmental features in English, providing useful explanations for them followed by extensive practice of them. These include syllables, word stress, sentence stress, phrasing, linking, prominence in discourse, intonation, and segmental features such as consonant and vowel sounds in English. These pronunciation features are structured around the following practical pronunciation goals:

GOALS

- to improve an understanding of pronunciation aspects in order for learners to build intelligible pronunciation skills and for teachers to use when teaching pronunciation aspects in the classroom
- to promote clear pronunciation skills for effective communication, with the understanding that intelligible, not native-like, pronunciation is essential and realistic for most learners and teachers of English
- to have students be aware of pronunciation aspects that are key to intelligibility and practice them
- to invite learners to monitor their speech, identify their own pronunciation errors and practice them on their own, taking responsibility for their pronunciation changes
- to increase self-confidence and reduce anxiety when listening to and speaking English

Organization of the Text

In *Sounds Clear*, suprasegmental and segmental pronunciation targets are organized around nine chapters. Chapter 1 addresses syllables in English and provides practice of how to identify them. Chapter 2 explores the characteristics of English stressed and unstressed syllables with practice. In Chapter 3, affecting factors and rules of English stress placements are introduced with the identification and production practice of stressed and unstressed syllables. Chapter 4 is designed to practice characteristic rhythm patterns in English, while Chapter 5 offers accounts for phrasing and linking with practice activities. In Chapter 6, the prominence in discourse is addressed, and then exercises to practice the identification and production of the most prominent words in discourse contexts are provided. In contrast, in Chapter 7, intonation patterns in English are explored with practice activities. Chapter 8 and 9 introduce English consonant and vowel sounds, respectively, with more of a focus on consonant and vowel sounds that many Korean-speaking learners of English often have troubles discriminating and pronouncing.

Organization within a Chapter

All chapters in this textbook adopt similar progression. Each chapter begins with "Background Information" which contains concepts, characteristics, and/or affecting factors of target pronunciation points to help learners promote linguistic knowledge about them. In the next section, "Listen" activities are presented to build awareness and improve aural skills of target features. "Pronunciation Tip" provides some useful tips for target features, including differences between Korean and English sound systems and the causes of difficulties that learners of English have in perceiving and pronouncing the target features. The next section includes "Listen and Speak" activities designed to relate aural to oral skills of target features and enhance self- and peer monitoring skills. "Listen and Speak" activities are followed by "Speak" activities in which target features are integrated with speaking formats that move from structured to more spontaneous tasks. Structured "Speak" activities intend to help learners gain control of target features with more focus on accuracy, while more spontaneous activities are designed to bridge the gap between a focus on accuracy and a focus on meaning in more communicative contexts.

Audio Files

The Audio Files present all listening activities marked *Track* with numbers.

Practice Activity Answer Keys

You will find Answer Keys for the activities at the back of the textbook.

To the Student

Even when English learners speak with noticeable nonnative patterns of English pronunciation, often called foreign accents, verbal communication can be successful. Many specialists and practitioners believe that intelligibility, not the entire elimination of foreign accents, should be the goal of second language pronunciation learning and teaching. Foreign accents are natural and inevitable characteristics of learning any new language, and there is nothing wrong with foreign accents, if they do not undermine pronunciation intelligibility. Moreover, foreign accents offer some clues about who you are and where you may be from. In this textbook, pronunciation training is not designed to eradicate all of your foreign accents but to improve your pronunciation intelligibility so that you can communicate comfortably and confidently with other speakers. This training can help you break down English pronunciation into small, manageable elements and help you practice target pronunciation aspects to the extent that listeners can easily understand your speech.

This textbook has been designed to make the daunting task of learning and teaching pronunciation doable. Regardless of whether you are studying individually, and/or taking classes, this book will enable you to get more out of your English learning. The accounts and explanations that are provided in this textbook intend to help you build linguistic knowledge about target pronunciation features, differences between Korean and English sound systems and difficulties you may encounter while learning English, improving your understandings and clearing up many misunderstandings about English pronunciation. Practices include both listening and speaking exercises and they proceed from structured activities with a focus on the control of new pronunciation points to more spontaneous, real-life communication tasks. Incorporated within most of the dialogs are clear and concise English phrases and expressions which are intended to equip learners and teachers alike with the language required of them not only in the classroom but in everyday life.

You will have opportunities to work individually, with partners, in small groups and as a class to take on speaker and listener roles. As a speaker, you will improve your ability to speak with clear and intelligible pronunciation. At the same time, as a listener, you will advance your capabilities to discriminate between clear and unclear pronunciation points in your classmates' speeches and to monitor and correct your pronunciation and the pronunciation of your classmates. It may be that it takes longer to improve your oral skills. To change your speech, you need to practice regularly, monitor your pronunciation more carefully, and keep trying out your new pronunciation skills both in isolation and in communicative contexts. The one who takes strong initiative and makes every effort to improve their pronunciation will make the most progress. No pain, no gain!

Audio Files

The Audio Files present all listening activities marked *Track* with numbers.

Practice Activity Answer Keys

You will find Answer Keys for the activities at the back of the textbook.

Guide to the Symbols

The following guide demonstrates the symbols used to represent different aspects of pronunciation.

STRESS

‹ Stressed Syllables

Stressed syllables in words are capitalized.

> PENcil, CLASSroom, HANDsome

‹ Strong Stress and Light Stress

In words of more than three syllables, two levels of stress are often shown in the same words. In these words, the syllable with a strong stress (primary stress) is indicated by capital letters and in bold, and the syllable with a light stress (secondary stress) is represented by capital letters and in italic.

> *E*du**CATE**, *E*co**NO**mical, *IN*di**CATE**

In phonetic transcription, strongly stressed syllables are represented with /ˈ/ at the beginning of them, while lightly stressed syllables are represented with /ˌ/ at the beginning of them.

> /ˌɛdʒʊˈkeyt/, /ˌɛkəˈnɑmɪkəl/, /ˌɪndəˈkeyt/

UNSTRESS

Unstressed syllables in words of more than one syllable are left unmarked.

> CHOrus, eRAser, forGET, deLIver

Reduced vowels in unstressed syllables are sometimes shown with the schwa vowel /ə/.

> at<u>o</u>m at<u>o</u>mic
> /ə/ /ə/
>
> maj<u>o</u>r maj<u>o</u>rity
> /ə/ /ə/

Sounds dropped in unstressed syllables are sometimes represented with a short vertical line (-).

> choc̶olate, fam̶ily, b̶ecause

THOUGHT GROUPS

A thought group, which is marked with a pause in spoken English, is indicated by a double slash (//).

> Julie does not remember // where she placed her purse // in the house.

LINKING

An underline indicates the linking of the last sound of a word to the initial sound of the following word in a thought group.

> She picke<u>d up a</u> cup // <u>in a</u> cupboard.

INTONATION

Intonation is indicated by an arrow. A downward arrow shows pitch fall and an upward arrow indicates pitch rise.

> I **REAL**ly **LIKE** the **NEW GAR**den ↘.
> Do you **WANT** to **WATCH** a **MO**vie ↗?

Steps and glides of falling intonation at the end of words are sometimes represented by lines.

> Glide: That's why I like those pants.
> Step: I will plant them in the garden.

PROMINENCE IN DISCOURSE

In a phrase or a sentence, the word which receives the most highlight, that is the prominence, has a dot over it.

> Was it a **LONG** *IN*tro**DUC**tion?
>
> No, it was a **SHORT** one.

CONSONANTS

Consonant sounds are represented with the following symbols between slash lines.

Symbols	Key Words	Symbols	Key Words
/p/	**p**in	/ʃ/	**p**ressure
/b/	**b**in	/ʒ/	**p**leasure
/t/	**t**ip	/h/	**h**igh
/d/	**d**ip	/tʃ/	**ch**in
/k/	**c**ap	/dʒ/	**j**in
/g/	**g**ap	/m/	**m**eat
/f/	**f**an	/n/	**n**eat
/v/	**v**an	/ŋ/	ki**ng**
/θ/	**th**igh	/l/	**l**ime
/ð/	**th**y	/r/	**r**ime
/s/	**s**ip	/y/	**y**oke
/z/	**z**ip	/w/	**w**oke

VOWELS

Vowel sounds are indicated with the following symbols between slash lines.

Symbols	Key Words	Symbols	Key Words
/iy/	b**ea**t	/uw/	b**oo**t
/ɪ/	b**i**t	/ʊ/	b**oo**k
/ey/	b**ai**t	/ow/	b**oa**t
/ɛ/	b**e**t	/ɔ/	b**ough**t
/æ/	b**a**t	/ɑ/	b**o**t
/ʌ/	b**u**t	/ay/	b**uy**
		/aw/	b**ow**
		/ɔy/	b**oy**

Chapter 1

SYLLABLES

 BACKGROUND INFORMATION

Q. What is a syllable?

A. A syllable is a part of a word that is pronounced as a unit. Syllables are the building blocks of words. For example, the word *permit* consists of two syllables, *per* and *mit*. Syllables can influence the stress, rhythm, and intonation patterns of English.

Q. How is a syllable structured?

A. It is made up of a single vowel with optional consonants. Within a syllable, a vowel takes up the position called the nucleus. The consonants before the vowel are referred to as the onset, while those after the vowel are called the coda. Onset and coda consonants tend to be optional, but the vowel must be present to form a syllable. The nucleus and the coda make up a unit called the rhyme in some languages.

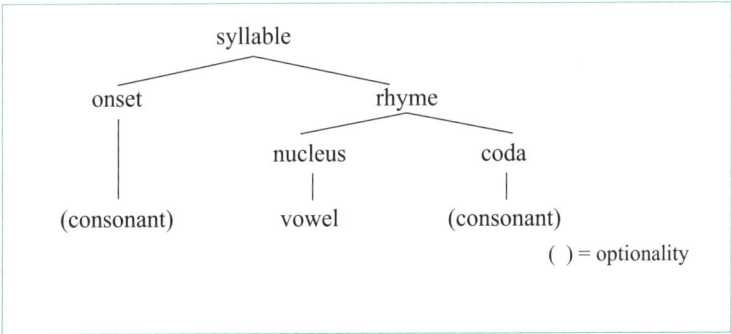

[Syllable Structure in Some Languages]

SYLLABLES 23

Q: Is rhyme frequently used in everyday life in English-speaking countries?

A: Yes, it is. Rhyme is a widely-used concept in poems, song lyrics, rap music, etc. Two syllables rhyme if they have identical nuclei and codas. The following is a famous limerick[1] which is known to have been composed by Edward Lear[2].

> There was an Old Man in a *tree*,
> Who was horribly bored by a *bee*.
> When they said, "Does it *buzz*?"
> He replied, "Yes, it *does*!
> It's a regular brute of a *bee*!"

In the limerick, *tree* and *bee* rhyme with the vowel /iy/, and *buzz* and *does* rhyme because they all end in /ʌz/.

Q. Do languages differ in the internal structure of syllables?

A. Yes, languages may differ in the internal structure of syllables. Let us compare the syllable structure of Korean and English as an example.

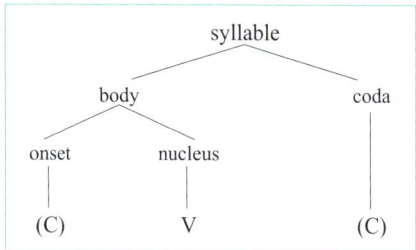 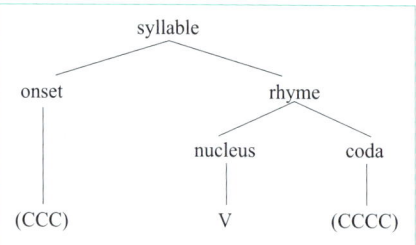

[Internal Structure of the Syllable in Korean]   [Internal Structure of the Syllable in English]

Korean has a left-branching body-coda structure. In the case of '강' meaning 'river' in Korean, many Koreans feel much more comfortable with the

---

1   A limerick is a humorous poem consisting of five lines. The first, second and fifth lines must have seven to ten syllables while rhyming and having the same verbal rhythm. The third and fourth lines should only have five to seven syllables and they too must rhyme with each other and have the same rhythm.
2   Edward Lear (1812~1888) was an English artist, illustrator, musician, author, and poet, known mostly for his literary nonsense in poetry and prose.

breakdown, '가' + 'ㅇ', than the breakdown, 'ㄱ' + 'ㅏ'. This indicates that the onset and the nucleus form a salient unit, or the body, in Korean. In contrast, for English speakers, the nucleus and the coda form a salient unit, or the rhyme, as illustrated in rhyming words in poems and stories and stress patterns in English. Languages may also differ in the number of consonants and the kind of consonants they allow in the syllable onset and coda. Korean permits only one consonant both in the onset and coda. In other words, no consonant clusters are allowed within a syllable in Korean. On the other hand, in English the number of consonants in the onset occuring at the beginning of a word ranges from one to three, whereas up to four consonants can occur in the coda at the end of a word.

Listen to the English words below. (Track 1-1)

Words	Word-initial Onset	Words	Word-final Coda
ray	/rey/	sick	/sɪk/
pray	/prey/	six	/sɪks/
spray	/sprey/	sixth	/sɪksθ/
		sixth's	/sɪksθs/

Partly because Korean does not allow consonant clusters in the onset and coda, Korean-speaking learners of English often add an extra vowel /ɨ/ (ㅡ in Korean character) or /i/ (ㅣ) between and after consonants in the clusters, changing the number of syllables of words. They also add an extra vowel /ɨ/ or /i/ even in English words ending in single coda consonants. The vowel /i/ is added mostly after the consonants /ʃ, ʒ, tʃ, dʒ/ and the vowel /ɨ/ after other consonants.

Words	English	Korean-accented
skip	/skɪp/	/sɨkɨpɨ/
mask	/mæsk/	/mæsɨkɨ/
belt	/bɛlt/	/bɛltɨ/
quiz	/kwɪz/	/kwɪzɨ/
bonus	/boʊnəs/	/boʊnəsɨ/
wished	/wɪʃt/	/wɪʃid/
village	/vɪlɪdʒ/	/vɪlɪdʒi/
bench	/bɛntʃ/	/bɛntʃi/

PRACTICE ACTIVITIES

 LISTEN 1 (Track 1-2)

Directions

1. Write the number of vowel letters in each word in the first column.
2. Listen to the words. Write the number of vowel sounds of each word in the second column and the number of syllables in the third column. Then, check your answers.

	Words	No. of Vowel Letters	No. of Vowel Sounds	No. of Syllables
Ex.	many	(1)	(2)	(2)
①	league	( )	( )	( )
②	cheese	( )	( )	( )
③	scrape	( )	( )	( )
④	hormone	( )	( )	( )
⑤	message	( )	( )	( )
⑥	gauge	( )	( )	( )
⑦	mystery	( )	( )	( )

Pronunciation Tip

The number of syllables of words typically matches the number of vowel sounds, not the number of vowel letters. When you count the number of syllables of a word, you should not confuse the number of syllables with the number of vowel letters. For example, the word *many* has one vowel letter, but it has two vowel sounds /æ/ and /i/, and two syllables. In contrast, the word *league* has four vowel letters, but it has only one vowel sound /iy/ and, therefore one syllable.

LISTEN 2 (Track 1-3)

Directions

Listen to the words in each pair. If the number of syllables is the same in the pair, mark *Same*. If different, mark *Different*. Then, check your answers.

	Words	Same	Different
Ex.	strike, fishy	☐	☑
①	belt, bench	☐	☐
②	quiz, skip	☐	☐
③	bonus, internet	☐	☐
④	manual, village	☐	☐
⑤	elevator, recreation	☐	☐
⑥	snack, mask	☐	☐
⑦	program, piano	☐	☐

LISTEN 3 (Track 1-4)

Directions

Listen and write the number of syllables of each word in the brackets. Then, check your answers.

	Words	No. of Syllables		Words	No. of Syllables
①	garage	( )	②	measure	( )
③	office	( )	④	lies	( )
⑤	improvement	( )	⑥	laughed	( )
⑦	ready	( )	⑧	research	( )
⑨	location	( )	⑩	minority	( )

LISTEN AND SPEAK (Track 1-5)

> **Directions**
>
> 1. Say the following limerick. Find the rhyming words and mark them.
> 2. Count the number of syllables in each line and write it in the blanks. Then, check your answers.
> 3. Listen to the limerick and repeat after the speaker.

Lines	Title: An Odd Fellow Named Gus	No. of Syllables
1	There was an odd fellow named Gus,	( )
2	When travelling he made such a fuss.	( )
3	He was banned from the train,	( )
4	Not allowed on a plane,	( )
5	And now travels only by bus.	( )

 SPEAK 1: Syllable Maze (Worksheet, p. 183)

> **Directions**
>
> 1. Find the path from the start to the finish by coloring words with two syllables. You can move from one square to the next horizontally or vertically but not diagonally.
> 2. Once finished, check your answers.

SPEAK 2: Counting Syllables

Directions

1. Complete the table with words matching the number of syllables indicated. You should have eight words in total, two words with 1, 2, 3, and 4 syllables each.
2. Get into pairs and take turns. Partner A reads each word to partner B in any order. Partner B says the number of syllables he/she hears. Look at the example.
3. Once finished, switch roles.

No. of Syllables	Words	
1	( )	( )
2	( )	( )
3	( )	( )
4	( )	( )

Example

You: belief
Your partner: Two syllables

SYLLABLES 29

SPEAK 3: Change the Lyrics

> **Directions**

1. Work in pairs or small groups.
2. Make new lyrics to the melody of the "Itsy Bitsy Spider" song. First, change the lyrics slightly (adjectives, adverbs, nouns) to make a new song. Look at the example (Version 1). Make sure each line has the same number of syllables as the original version.

Example (Version 1)

Original Lyrics	No. of Syllables	Changed Lyrics	No. of Syllables
The itsy bitsy spider	7	The ziggy zaggy zebra	7
Went up the waterspout	6	Ate up some grass and plants	6
Down came the rain and	5	Then came the rain and	5
Washed the spider out	5	Washed the zebra down	5
Out came the sun	4	Out came the sun	4
And dried up all the rain	6	And dried up all the rain	6
Now the itsy bitsy spider	8	Now the ziggy zaggy zebra	8
Went up the spout again	6	Is dry and clean again	6

Your Turn (Version 1)

Original Lyrics	No. of Syllables	Changed Lyrics	No. of Syllables
The itsy bitsy spider	7		
Went up the waterspout	6		
Down came the rain and	5		
Washed the spider out	5		
Out came the sun	4		
And dried up all the rain	6		
Now the itsy bitsy spider	8		
Went up the spout again	6		

3. Second, change the song entirely by picking a new topic and replacing each verse with new words. Look at the example (Version 2). Make sure each line has the same number of syllables as the original version.

Example (Version 2)

Original Lyrics	No. of Syllables	Changed Lyrics	No. of Syllables
The itsy bitsy spider	7	Class, is everyone finished?	7
Went up the waterspout	6	We need to pack up now	6
Down came the rain and	5	I won't give homework	5
Washed the spider out	5	Because you did well	5
Out came the sun	4	Return your books	4
And dried up all the rain	6	And pencils in the box	6
Now the itsy bitsy spider	8	You'll be very, very happy	8
Went up the spout again	6	To know it's time to go!	6

Your Turn (Version 2)

Original Lyrics	No. of Syllables	Changed Lyrics	No. of Syllables
The itsy bitsy spider	7		
Went up the waterspout	6		
Down came the rain and	5		
Washed the spider out	5		
Out came the sun	4		
And dried up all the rain	6		
Now the itsy bitsy spider	8		
Went up the spout again	6		

4. Once finished, sing your new songs out loud.

Chapter 2

STRESSED AND UNSTRESSED SYLLABLES

PART 1. STRESS

 BACKGROUND INFORMATION

Q. What is stress and what are the major characteristics of stressed syllables in English?

A. Stress can be defined as relative prominence. If you say all the syllables in a word, for example, *attention*, the second syllable of the word is sounded louder, longer, and higher-pitched because you say the second syllable with a greater amount of energy than the neighboring syllables. Also, the second syllable vowel is pronounced with full quality, whereas the vowels in the unstressed first and third syllables are reduced into the schwa vowel /ə/.[3] These characteristics make stressed syllables more salient than unstressed syllables.

Q. Why is word stress important to pronunciation intelligibility?

A. Mistakes in word stress may lead to misunderstandings in communication. Stress on the wrong syllable in a word can make the word difficult to hear and understand. Since stress change in words may lead to meaning change, stressing words accurately is critical to pronunciation intelligibility.

---

[3] The reduced vowel is pronounced 'uh' with the tongue in the rest position and represented with the symbol /ə/ called schwa. The schwa vowel is the most common vowel sound in English, mostly occurring in unstressed syllables.

🎧 Listen to the two-syllable words *message* and *massage* in the following context. (Track 2-1)

① She received a *MEssage* yesterday.
② She received a *masSAGE* yesterday.

Q. Do words in English have stress in a given position?

A. Some languages have stress in a given position. For example, in Czech the first syllable of a word always carries the primary stress (*HLAva* "head"), in French the last syllable is constantly stressed (*baGUETTE* "baguette"), and the second to last syllable is always the most prominent in Polish (*odTWOrzyć* "to replay"). On the other hand, in English, stress is not fixed to a given position. In some words, the first syllable is stressed, in other words, the second syllable is stressed, and still in others, the third syllable is stressed.

🎧 Listen to the English words below. (Track 2-2)

① **RES**taurant   **IN**terview
② con**SI**der   a**TO**mic
③ employ**EE**   pio**NEER**

Q. How many levels of stress are there in English?

A. In some three-syllable or longer words, there may be two different levels of stress. If you say the words below and tap on the stressed syllables, you will find that you can tap on the first and third syllable of the words with the third syllable carrying a greater degree of stress than the first syllable. These levels of stress are referred to as primary (strongly stressed) and secondary (lightly stressed). In these words, the second and fourth syllables are unstressed.

🎧 Listen to the words below. (Track 2-3)

*IL*lu**STRA**tion   *AD*ver**TISE**ment   *DIS*con**TI**nue

PRACTICE ACTIVITIES

LISTEN 1 (Track 2-4)

Directions

Listen to the prompts, paying close attention to the stressed syllables. Mark the pictures which signify the prompts. Then, check your answers.

① ☐ a.    ☐ b.

② ☐ a.    ☐ b.

③ ☐ a.    ☐ b.

④ ☐ a.    ☐ b.

STRESSED AND UNSTRESSED SYLLABLES   35

LISTEN 2 (Track 2-5)

Directions

Listen to the words in each pair, paying close attention to the strongly stressed syllables. If the stress is on the same syllable, mark *Same*. If it is on a different syllable, mark *Different*. Then, check your answers.

	Words	Same	Different
Ex.	damage, garage	☐	☑
①	patient, pleasure	☐	☐
②	delete, edit	☐	☐
③	appeal, apple	☐	☐
④	beautiful, delicious	☐	☐
⑤	consider, remember	☐	☐
⑥	possible, expensive	☐	☐
⑦	seriously, personally	☐	☐

 LISTEN 3 (Track 2-6)

Directions

Listen to the words and underline the strongly stressed syllable. Then, check your answers.

Ex. <u>sum</u> mer

① of fi cial
② im me di ate
③ at mos phere
④ re com mend
⑤ as sign ment
⑥ com pe ti tive
⑦ en cou rage
⑧ ma jo ri ty
⑨ e le gant

PART 2. UNSTRESS

 BACKGROUND INFORMATION

Q. What are the main characteristics of unstressed syllables in English?

A. Unstressed syllables are pronounced less prominently than stressed syllables. They are typically lower-pitched, shorter, and quieter than stressed syllables. In addition, vowels in unstressed syllables are often weakened into schwa /ə/. The vowel weakening in unstressed syllables helps create the alternating rhythm pattern of stressed and unstressed syllables in English. Also, in words, some sounds in unstressed syllables may be dropped entirely.

Listen to the words below. (Track 2-7)

Vowel Weakening	Dropping
PENcil /ə/	CHOC~~o~~late
baNAna /ə/ /ə/	AVerage
MENded /ə/	~~th~~em
	~~be~~CAUSE

Q. Is the weakening of unstressed syllables important to pronunciation intelligibility?

A. Yes and no, depending on who you are speaking to. Any stressed syllable in English can have a full vowel, but a syllable with a weakened vowel may not have stress. The reduced vowel quality and low-pitched, short, and quiet features of unstressed syllables are significant for native speakers of English to perceive and produce words and phrases. Confusions will arise for native speakers of English with errors in which stress is correctly assigned but an expected reduced vowel is produced as a full vowel. In other words, the absence of reduced vowels in unstressed syllables may be damaging to pronunciation intelligibility in communication with native speakers of English. On the other hand, the weakening of vowels in unstressed syllables may not be beneficial to communication among nonnative speakers of English. Nonnative speakers of English may expect full vowels in unstressed syllables and have difficulties recovering full vowels from reduced vowels. This means that weakened forms may reduce pronunciation intelligibility in communication between nonnatives.

⭐ PRACTICE ACTIVITIES

 LISTEN 1 (Track 2-8)

Directions

Listen to the words in each pair and underline the reduced vowels in each word. Then, check your answers.

Ex.	e le ment	e le men ta ry
①	a tom	a to mic
②	ra pid	ra pi di ty
③	e dit	e di tion
④	pre fer	pre fe rence
⑤	a ble	a bi li ty
⑥	bo ta ny	bo ta ni cal

 LISTEN 2 (Track 2-9)

Directions

Listen to the words. Strike out the dropped sounds. Then, check your answers.

Ex.	weaken				
①	about	②	camera	③	tomorrow
④	finally	⑤	sudden	⑥	probably
⑦	different	⑧	enough	⑨	cousin

SPEAK 1: Word Stress Bingo (Worksheet, p. 185)

Directions

1. Read each word and draw the stress pattern next to it individually. Then, check your answers.

	Words	Stress Pattern		Words	Stress Pattern
Ex.	present (noun)	● ○		present (verb)	○ ●
①	ice cream			I scream	
②	selfish			sell fish	
③	minute			minute	
④	Korea			career	
⑤	history			his story	
⑥	decade			decayed	
⑦	August			august	
⑧	pronouns			pronounce	
⑨	Adam			a dam	
⑩	address (n)			address (v)	

2. ⓐ Work in pairs or small groups.
   ⓑ Complete your bingo grid with the words or phrases from the box above. Put only one word/phrase in each box.
   ⓒ Then, take turns calling out words, highlighting the stressed syllables and weakening the unstressed syllables.
   ⓓ Cross out the word or phrase you hear. If you cross out four blanks in a row in any direction, you have one bingo.
   ⓔ The first person to get three bingos is the winner.

STRESSED AND UNSTRESSED SYLLABLES 39

SPEAK 2: Highlighting and Weakening Syllables

Directions

1. Underline the stressed syllables and strike out the dropped sounds individually. Then, check your answers.

A	B
f a m i l y	f a m i l y
b a k e r y	b a k e r y
a n o t h e r	a n o t h e r
t a k e n	t a k e n
f a v o r i t e	f a v o r i t e
v e g e t a b l e	v e g e t a b l e
i n s t e a d	i n s t e a d
a r r i v e	a r r i v e
g a r a g e	g a r a g e
c a m e r a	c a m e r a

2. ⓐ Work in pairs.
   ⓑ Partner A reads the first five words out loud. Partner B reads the last five words out loud. Highlight the stressed syllables and drop the missing sounds in unstressed syllables.
   ⓒ When finished, switch roles.

3. Read the passage below out loud, highlighting the stressed syllables and weakening the unstressed syllables. Then, check the example answer.

When you arrive at my apartment, you will see my favorite bakery and a small mart that sells fresh vegetables on your left. If you have a car, you can park in the garage. If the elevator is taken, use the stairs instead. Another thing to mention is that there is a security camera at the entrance. But don't worry, my family will be around to meet you.

SPEAK 3: Role-Play Situations

Directions

1. Work in pairs.
2. Choose a role-play situation and write a script.
3. Practice your role-play aloud. Highlight stressed syllables and weaken unstressed syllables.
4. Once finished, show the class the role-play.
5. (Optional) Record your role-play and annotate your script. Compare if you highlighted stressed syllables and weakened unstressed syllables.

Situations

Situation 1: At the Restaurant

You go to a restaurant with your younger sibling, and you are the only one with money. The food is horrible, but you have already started eating the food. The owner hands you the bill, but you refuse to pay. You argue.

Situation 2: The Toilet

You are at your boyfriend/girlfriend's place. You need to use the bathroom, but you are too shy. You ask them to leave the house for a while, but they refuse. How will you persuade them to leave? You have an interesting conversation.

Situation 3: At the Gym

You are exercising at your local gym. A really good-looking girl/guy walks in, and you want to impress them by pushing weights, but the weights are too heavy, and they hit your head, and you are embarrassed. They ask you if you need help, but you want to act brave. You have an interesting conversation.

Situation 4: The Break-up

You have been wining and dining a girl you like, hoping she will become your girl. But she calls you and tells you she doesn't want to be your girlfriend, so now you want your money back. How will you convince her?

Situation 5: The Ski Resort

You go to a food court. You see a table and head over to it, but an older person steals your seat and tells you to look elsewhere. You get angry and argue.

Situation 6: A Free Gift

You ask someone for something expensive, hoping they give it to you for free because they don't use it. But they ask you to pay for it. You have an interesting conversation with them.

Situation 7: The Bar

You are at the bar and see a foreigner you like, but you don't know how to speak English. You have a weird conversation.

Situation 8: Happy Wife, Happy Life

You're playing computer games, and your wife asks you if she's gained weight. No matter what you say, she still gets angry at you. You try not to get in trouble.

Role-Play

Situation: _____

A: _____

B: _____

A: _____

B: _____

A: _____

B: _____

A: _____

B: _____

A: _____

B: _____

Chapter 3
PREDICTABLE WORD STRESS

   BACKGROUND INFORMATION

Q. Are stress placements in English words predictable?

A. Mostly, yes. Native speakers of English tend to know which syllable receives the primary stress even when they encounter non-English words. Let us consider three-syllable non-English words, *GiGONdas*, *ZaVENtem*, and *TaVOla* borrowed from Carr (1999)[4]. A majority of native English speakers stress the second syllable to the last. Is their stress placement on the penultimate syllable by accident or is it because of existing stress patterns? The answer to this question seems to be the latter. Native English speakers are likely to stress the three non-English words using existing stress patterns in English words such as *aGENdas*, *moMENtum*, and *eBOla*. However, English stress patterns are not as straightforward as languages such as Czech and French where stress is assigned to a given position in words. In English, several elements factor in stress placements, which makes stress placements in English less transparent and more complicated.

Q. What factors affect stress patterns in English?

A. Stress placements in English words are affected by factors such as syllable weight (light vs. heavy), word category (nouns/adjectives vs. verbs), word formation (words with affixes, compounds, and phrasal nouns and verbs), and spelling patterns (words spelled alike, number words, words containing *-self*, words ending in *-ate,* and consonants + *y*).

---

4   Carr, Philip. 1999. *English Phonetics and Phonology: An Introduction*. Malden, MA: Blackwell Publishers Ltd.

PART 1. STRESS PATTERNS ACCORDING TO SYLLABLE WEIGHT AND WORD CATEGORY

PRACTICE ACTIVITIES

 LISTEN 1 (Track 3-1)

Directions

Listen to the words, paying close attention to the stressed syllables. Underline the stressed syllable for each word. Then, check your answers.

Ex. a <u>loud</u>

① as sign ② di vorce ③ be low
④ hea vy ⑤ so fa ⑥ de ny
⑦ con sist ⑧ cor rect ⑨ e rase

Pronunciation Tip

Syllable Weight

In English, syllables can be divided into two types, light and heavy. A syllable is regarded as heavy if it is made up of a tense vowel, a diphthong, or a tense or lax vowel with a coda consonant. On the other hand, it is considered light if it includes lax vowels without any coda consonant. In English words, light syllables or syllables with schwa are generally unstressed, whereas stressed syllables are likely to be heavy ones. In words, for example, *beLOW* /bəˈloʊ/ and *reSIST* /rəˈzɪst/, the second syllable is heavy, being composed of a tense vowel and a lax vowel followed by two consonants, respectively, and it is stressed. On the other hand, the first syllable being made up of schwa is light and unstressed.

Weight	Stressed	Weight	Unstressed
Heavy Syllables	• Syllables with a tense vowel or a diphthong • Syllables with a vowel and (a) coda consonant(s)	Light Syllables	• Syllables with a lax vowel without any consonants
		Light/ Heavy Syllables	• Syllables with schwa /ə/ • Syllables with schwa /ə/ and (a) consonant(s)

LISTEN 2 (Track 3-2)

Directions

Listen to the words, paying close attention to the stressed syllables. Underline the stressed syllable for each word. Then, check your answers.

① mo ment
② mu se um
③ ex pect
④ pa tient
⑤ so lid
⑥ at tend
⑦ e dit
⑧ si lence
⑨ tic ket

 LISTEN 3 (Track 3-3)

Directions

Listen to the sentences, paying close attention to the stress pattern of the words in the brackets. Underline the stressed syllables of the words in the brackets. Then, check your answers.

① a. Did you see the (sus pect)?
   b. I (sus pect) they cheated on the exam.

② a. Bill needs to (pro ject) his voice tomorrow.
   b. I should finish the (pro ject) by tomorrow.

③ a. I need to get a (re fund) for this product.
   b. We can't (re fund) the item after the expiry date.

④ a. They sell quality (pro duces).
   b. It (pro duces) a large amount of gas.

⑤ a. He's going to (re cord) a new song.
   b. There's no (re cord) of them in the archive.

> **Pronunciation Tip**

Word Category

Word categories, or parts of speech, influence stress placements in English. In the case of two-syllable nouns/adjectives and verbs, the final syllable tends to receive stress if it is a heavy syllable with a tense vowel or a diphthong regardless of whether it is closed by consonants or not.

Nouns/Adjectives	Verbs
toDAY	deLAY
beLIEF	eRASE
uNIQUE	arRIVE

However, two-syllable nouns/adjectives and verbs in English react differently to consonants at the end of words. In the case of nouns/adjectives, coda consonants in the last syllable tend to be ignored in entirety, while only the last consonant of the final syllable in verbs tends to be ignored for stress placement. So, stress tends to be assigned to the first syllable of two-syllable nouns/adjectives, while the final syllable in two-syllable verbs tends to receive stress if it is closed by more than one consonant. The noun/adjective-verb difference in treating word-final consonants yields the asymmetric distributional pattern that two-syllable nouns tend to have stress on the first syllable, while two-syllable verbs tend to have stress on the second syllable.

	Nouns/Adjectives	Verbs
Closed by one consonant	BROther	WHISper
	TAble	FInish
	QUIet	Edit
Closed by more than one consonant	PArent	seLECT
	Orange	reLAX
	FREquent	arRANGE

This asymmetric pattern of stress in two-syllable nouns/adjectives and verbs also accounts for stress assignment in noun-verb pairs which are spelled alike.

Nouns	Verbs
PROgress	pro**GRESS**
PERmit	per**MIT**
INsult	in**SULT**
CONduct	con**DUCT**

The stress pattern of two-syllable nouns/adjectives and verbs can be summarized as below.

Stress on the First Syllable	Stress on the Last Syllable
• Most 2 syllable nouns • Most 2 syllable adjectives	• Most 2 syllable verbs

 SPEAK 1: Airport Check-in

Directions

1. Work in pairs.
2. Partner A will be the check-in agent and partner B will be the passenger. Take turns asking questions below about the check-in process at the airport.
3. Use the passenger information below to help you answer.
4. When finished, switch roles.

Questions

① Where are you flying to today?
② May I see your passport and ticket, please?
③ Are you checking in any luggage?
④ Have you left your luggage unattended at any time?
⑤ Has anyone asked you to bring anything on the flight?
⑥ Would you like a window, aisle, or middle seat?
⑦ Do you have any of these prohibited items? A Swiss knife, a lighter, explosives...
⑧ Here is your boarding pass. Go through security and your flight to (*country*) will depart from gate (*number*) at (*time*).

Passenger Information

Destination	Gate & Flight Time	Baggage	Seating
China	Gate 102/ 5:50 pm	1 suitcase and a carry-on	Window
Sweden	Gate 45/ 3:15 pm	2 suitcases and a carry-on	Middle
Thailand	Gate 26/ 2:00 pm	A carry-on only	Window
Kenya	Gate 130/ 12:00 pm	2 suitcases and a backpack	Anything
Qatar	Gate 22/ 7:45 am	3 suitcases	Aisle

 SPEAK 2: Have You Ever…? (Word Bank & Worksheet, p. 187)

Directions

1. Complete the sentences using the words in the word bank.
2. Mark the stressed syllable for each word.
3. Walk around the classroom and ask your classmates, "Have you ever…?", for example, "Have you ever written a novel?"
4. If you find somebody who answers "Yes, I have," write down their name. You must have a different name in each box.
5. Try to talk to as many different people as possible.

PART 2. STRESS PATTERNS IN MORPHOLOGICALLY COMPLEX WORDS

PRACTICE ACTIVITIES

 LISTEN 1 (Track 3-4)

Directions

Listen to the words, paying close attention to the stressed syllables. Underline the strongly stressed syllable for each word. Then, check your answers.

① dis ap point
② re in form
③ mis ad vise
④ ex- mem ber
⑤ in doors
⑥ im pos si ble
⑦ a mo ral
⑧ un plea sant
⑨ de me rit
⑩ en dan ger

Pronunciation Tip

Prefix

When a prefix, for example, *dis-*, *re-*, *mis-*, *ex-*, *in-*, *im-*, *a-*, *un- de- en-*, etc., is added to a root, the stress of the root word does not change.

Prefixes	Meaning/Function	Roots	Prefixed Words
dis-	opposite of	apPOINT	disapPOINT
re-	again	inFORM	reinFORM
mis-	wrongly, unsuitably	adVISE	misadVISE
ex-	indicate a former title/status	MEMber	ex-MEMber
in-	in, within	DOORS	inDOORS
im-	opposite of, not	POSsible	imPOSsible
a-	without, not	MOral	aMOral
un-	opposite of, not	PLEAsant	unPLEAsant
de-	opposite of, not	MErit	deMErit
en-	put into or onto something	DANger	enDANger

PREDICTABLE WORD STRESS

LISTEN 2 (Track 3-5)

Directions

Listen to the words, paying close attention to the stressed syllables. Underline the strongly stressed syllable for each word. Then, check your answers.

① mem ber ship   ② po wer less   ③ de pen ding
④ won der ful   ⑤ tra ve ler   ⑥ na tu ral
⑦ ea ger ly   ⑧ neigh bor hood ⑨ ug li ness
⑩ com for ta ble

Pronunciation Tip

Neutral Suffix

In the case of words formed by adding some suffixes such as *-ship*, *-less*, *ing*, *-ful*, *-e/or*, *-al*, *-ly*, *-hood*, *-ness*, *-able,* etc., the stress pattern of the root in suffixed words remains the same as the stress pattern of the unsuffixed root.

Suffixes	Meaning/Function	Roots	Suffixed Words
-ship	form nouns of state or condition	MEMber	MEMbership
-less	without	POwer	POwerless
-ing	express the action of the verbs or its results	dePEND	dePENding
-ful	have a quantity that would fill something named	WONder	WONderful
-e/or	designate a person or a thing that performs a specified action	TRAvel	TRAveler
-al	of the kind, pertaining to	NAture	NAtural
-ly	form adverbs/adjectives from adjectives/nouns	EAger	EAgerly
-hood	denote state, condition, character, etc., or a body of persons of a particular character or class	NEIGHbor	NEIGHborhood

-ness	form abstract nouns denoting quality and state	UGly	UGliness
-able	form adjectives with the meaning of "capable of", "susceptible of", or "fit for"	COMfort	COMfortable

LISTEN 3 (Track 3-6)

Directions

Listen to the words, paying close attention to the stressed syllables. Underline the strongly stressed syllable for each word. Then, check your answers.

① e co no mi cal   ② mo ti va tion   ③ ra pi di ty
④ mys te ri ous   ⑤ per so ni fy   ⑥ co me di an
⑦ e co lo gy   ⑧ en gi neer   ⑨ em ploy ee
⑩ mil lio naire   ⑪ car too nesque ⑫ Chi nese

Pronunciation Tip

Non-neutral Suffix

As discussed above, the addition of some suffixes does not change the stress pattern in root words. However, there are other suffixes, for example, *-ian, -ic(al), -ify, -ion, -i/eous, -ity, -ogy, aire, -ee, -eer, -ese, -esque*, etc., which tend to shift the stress in the root when they are suffixed to the root words. Among these words, stress pattern varies in two ways: Suffixes, for example, *-ian, -ic(al), -ify, -ion, -i/eous, -ity, -ogy*, etc., cause the root stress to shift to the syllable right before the suffix.

Suffixes	Meanings or Functions	Roots	Suffixed Words
-(i)an	form nouns from words ending in *-ic* or *-y* with the meaning of "one who belongs to" or "one who relates to"	COmedy CAnada	coMEdian CaNAdian

-ic(al)	form adjectives from nouns with the meaning of "of" or "pertaining to"	e**CO**nomy	eco**NO**mical
-ify	form verbs with the meaning of "to make", "cause to be" or "render"	**PER**son	per**SO**nify
-ion	form nouns from verbs to denote action or condition	**MO**tivate	moti**VA**tion
-i/eous	form adjectives with the sense of "possessing", "full of" or "a given quality"	**MY**stery	mys**TER**ious
-ity	form abstract nouns expressing state or condition	**RA**pid	ra**PI**dity
-ogy	form nouns with the meaning of "field of study" or "discipline"	**E**co	e**CO**logy

On the other hand, suffixes such as *-aire*, *-ee*, *-eer*, *-ese*, *-esque*, etc., which are borrowed into English via French, attract the stress to the final syllable of suffixed words.

Suffixes	Meanings or Functions	Roots	Suffixed Words
-aire	form nouns denoting a person characterized by or occupied with that named by the root	**MIL**lion	millio**NAIRE**
-ee	form nouns meaning a person or thing that is the object of that verb	em**PLOY**	employ**EE**
-eer	form nouns denoting persons	**EN**gine	engi**NEER**
-ese	form adjectives of place names, especially countries or cities	**POR**tugal	Portu**GUESE**
-esque	mean "like" or "resembling"	**PIC**ture	pictu**RESQUE**

LISTEN 4 (Track 3-7)

Directions

Listen to the compound words, paying close attention to the stressed syllables. Underline the strongly stressed syllable for each word. Then, check your answers.

① yel low jac ket
② ear ring
③ green house
④ lip stick
⑤ rea dy-made
⑥ smoke-free
⑦ se cond hand
⑧ mid dle-aged
⑨ hand write
⑩ ba by sit
⑪ test-drive (verb)
⑫ dou ble-click

Pronunciation Tip

Compounds

Stress pattern in compound words varies depending on their word categories. In the case of compound nouns which are mainly created by attaching an adjective or a noun to a noun, stress is placed on the first part of compound nouns with no regard to their composition.

	Adjective-Noun	Noun-Noun
Compound Nouns	YELlow jacket GREENhouse	EARring LIPstick

On the other hand, as for compound adjectives and compound verbs, stress usually goes to the second element, if any of the parts is not a noun. If one of the parts is a noun, primary stress tends to be placed on that noun.

	With Noun	Without Noun
Compound Adjectives	SMOKE-free secondHAND	ready-MADE middle-AGED
Compound Verbs	HANDwrite BAbysit	double-CLICK test-DRIVE (verb)

However, compound adjectives exhibit two stress patterns, depending on their position in a sentence. If a compound adjective precedes a noun, modifying the noun, the first part in the compound tends to receive stress. On the other hand, if a compound adjective comes at the end of an utterance, the second part of the compound tends to be stressed.

He is a **GOOD**-looking man.　　The man is good **LOO**king.

This is a **WELL**-trained dog.　　The dog is well-**TRAINED**.

LISTEN 5 (Track 3-8)

Directions

Listen to the sentences, paying close attention to the stress pattern of the phrasal words in the brackets. Underline the stressed syllables of the words in the brackets. Then, check your answers.

① a. Some students (drop out) in the middle of the semester.
   b. The (drop-out) rates were the highest last year.

② a. They'll (pay back) the loss as soon as they return home.
   b. I'll use my (payback) points for this purchase.

③ a. The new development is a remarkable (breakthrough).
   b. You should (break through) some barriers to finish this project.

④ a. The town has a (bypass) which keeps traffic out of the center.
   b. They (passed by) the museum on the way to the park.

⑤ a. I hope they don't (break up) over this matter.
   b. A (breakup) always hurts.

⑥ a. She (hands out) the cakes at snack time.
   b. There's a lady distributing (handouts) on Main Street.

⑦ a. (Make up) your mind before you leave for Chicago.
b. I'll have (makeup) classes next week.

⑧ a. They'll (break down) the house next month.
b. The week-by-week (breakdown) helps their training.

Pronunciation Tip

Phrasal Nouns and Verbs

Phrasal words consist of two or three words, usually composed of verbs followed by adverbial particles and/or prepositions. They can be used either as verbs or nouns. In the case of phrasal verbs, stress goes to adverbial particles. On the other hand, in the case of phrasal nouns, stress goes to the first component.

SPEAK 1: College Life Dice Bingo (Worksheet, p. 189)

Direction

1. Work in pairs or small groups of 3 or 4.
2. Roll the dice twice to find your question. The 1st roll determines the column. The 2nd roll determines the row.
3. Talk for one or two minutes about your question. Your classmates can ask you follow-up questions. Once you have answered a question, cross it out.

   Follow-up Questions
   - Can you tell me more?
   - Why do you think so?

4. If a question has already been answered, you cannot play and must give your dice to the next player.
5. The first person to get three bingo lines in any direction wins.

PREDICTABLE WORD STRESS

SPEAK 2: The Perfect Date Survey (Worksheet, p. 191)

Direction

1. Complete the survey about yourself.
2. Interview four other people and write their answers in columns 1-4.
3. After each answer, ask a follow-up question to find out more about your interviewee.

Follow-up Questions

- Why do you think that?
- Can you tell me more?

4. Work in small groups of 4 or 5. Take turns asking and answering questions about the Perfect Date Survey. Use the answers from the survey to help you.

Follow-up Questions

- What do you have for question _____?
  (or What's your answer for question _____?)
- Who are you most like?
- Who are you least like?
- Who is the most interesting person you interviewed?
  (or Who surprised you the most?)

PART 3. STRESS PATTERNS ACCORDING TO SPELLING

⭐ PRACTICE ACTIVITIES

 LISTEN 1 (Track 3-9)

Directions

Listen to the words, paying close attention to the stress pattern of the words. Underline the strongly stressed syllable for each word. Then, check your answers.

① four teen
② se ven ty
③ him self
④ our selves
⑤ ap pre ci ate
⑥ gra du ate
⑦ re fri ge rate
⑧ ne go ti ate
⑨ phar ma cy
⑩ his tory

Pronunciation Tip

Stress in Number Words, -*self* Words, Verbs Ending in -*ate*, and Words Ending in Consonant+*y*

- Number words ending in -*teen* and -*ty* have a predictable stress pattern. Words ending in -*teen* have stress on the -*teen* syllable, while those ending in -*ty* have stress on the first syllable.
- Words containing -*self* and -*selves* have stress on themselves.
- In three-syllable or four-syllable words ending in -*ate* and consonant+*y*, stress is usually placed on the third syllable from the end of the words.
- Verbs ending in –*ate* are pronounced like the word *eight* (e.g., *I will graduate next year*, *Can you estimate the cost?*), while nouns, adjectives, and adverbs are pronounced like the word *it* (e.g., *I am a graduate, Can I have an estimate?*)

SPEAK 1: Ty & Teen Snakes and Ladders (Worksheet, p. 193)

> **Directions**
>
> 1. Work in pairs or small groups of 4.
> 2. Each player puts their counter on the space that says 'Start'.
> 3. Toss a coin. Heads moves one space and tails moves two spaces. If your counter lands at the bottom of a ladder, you can move up to the top of the ladder. If your counter lands on the head of a snake, you must slide down to the snake's tail.
> 4. Say the answer out loud. For example, 50 - 20 is 30.
> 5. The first player to finish is the winner.

 SPEAK 2: Personality Interview

> **Directions**
>
> 1. Work in pairs.
> 2. Interview each other to find out how similar and different you are.
> 3. Write five sentences to summarize your findings.

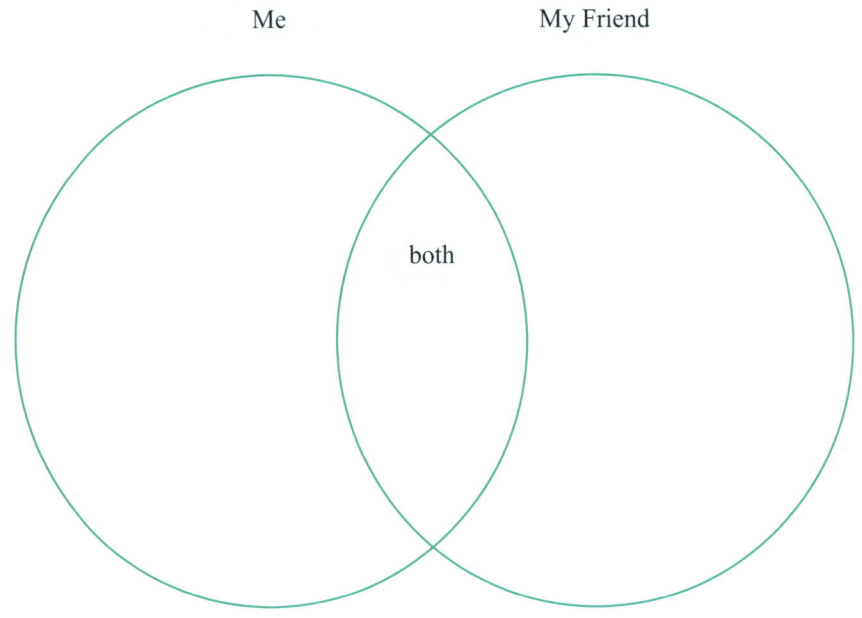

Word Bank

Strengths	Weaknesses
reliable	procrastinate
honest	self-critical
hardworking	insecure
team player	ultrasensitive
taking initiative	easy to get demotivated
creative	overthinker
versatile	slacker
dedicated	short attention span
punctual	unreliable
brainiac	inconsistent
idea person	undisciplined
overachiever	impulsive

_____

_____

_____

_____

_____

Chapter 4

RHYTHM IN SENTENCES

BACKGROUND INFORMATION

Q. Does English have a characteristic rhythm pattern?

A. Yes, it does. In English words and sentences, stressed and unstressed syllables alternate with the stressed syllables occurring at a regular time interval. The number of syllables varies in the following sentences, but the number of stressed syllables is the same. Listen to the sentences below.

 Listen and tap the rhythm of the stressed syllables. (Track 4-1)

	No. of Stresses	No. of Syllables
SINGing a FUNny SONG, SONG,	4	7
I was GOing aLONG, LONG, LONG.	4	8
The LANE that I WENT was so LONG, LONG.	4	9
And the SONG that I SUNG was as LONG, LONG.	4	10

In the first sentence, four syllables are stressed and are said longer than the stressed syllables in the following three sentences in which the number of the unstressed syllables increases. In sentences, the more unstressed syllables there are between stressed syllables, the shorter the stressed syllables, and the unstressed syllables are pronounced to maintain approximately the same time interval between the stressed syllables. English is classified as a stress-timed language because the number of stressed syllables determines the length of an utterance. On the other hand, in a syllable-timed language as in Korean in which the time needed to say each syllable is roughly equivalent, the length of an utterance depends on the number of syllables.

Q. What are trochaic and iambic rhythms?

A. Trochaic rhythm is the grouping of successive beats into pairs in which the first beat is more prominent. In contrast, iambic rhythm is the grouping of beats into pairs with the second beat more prominent.

Listen and tap the rhythm of the stressed syllables. (Track 4-2)

Trochaic Pattern (● ○)	Iambic Pattern (○ ●)
SISters ANswers WINdows	eRASE prePARE apPEAL
LOVEly SISters	eRASE the SCRIBbles
FInal ANswers	prePARE the MEAL
Open WINdows	apPEAL to the COURT

Q. Are there any types of words that tend to receive stress in sentences?

A. Yes, there are. Words that carry the most meaning are stressed in English sentences. These words are referred to as content words, which include nouns, main verbs, adjectives, adverbs, negative words, wh-question words, numerals, etc. On the other hand, words that carry little to no meaning but are important to the sentence's grammatical structure are not stressed if they are not given special attention. They are called function or structure words, which include articles, pronouns, prepositions, relative/demonstrative pronouns, auxiliary verbs, conjunctions, etc.

Content Words	Function Words
Nouns	Articles
Main verbs	Auxiliary verbs
Adjectives	Conjunctions
Adverbs	Determiners
Negative words	Prepositions
Wh-question words	Pronouns
Number words	Relative/Demonstrative pronouns

Function words without stress are often reduced in various forms in English.

Function Words	Reduced Forms
and	/ənd/, /ən/, /n/
has	/həz/, /əz/, /z/, /s/
would	/wəd/, /əd/, /d/
him/them	/əm/
your	/yə/

PRACTICE ACTIVITIES

 LISTEN 1 (Track 4-3)

Directions

Listen to the story of the Ugly Duckling. Count the number of the stressed words in each line and write it in the brackets. Then, check your answers.

Lines	THE UGLY DUCKLING	No. of Stresses
①	A farmer had a duck which laid ten eggs.	( )
②	Soon, they all hatched.	( )
③	Of the ten, nine ducklings looked like the mom.	( )
④	The tenth one was big, gray and ugly.	( )
⑤	All the other ducklings made fun of the ugly one.	( )
⑥	Unhappy in the farm, the poor duckling ran away to a river nearby.	( )
⑦	There he sees white, beautiful swans.	( )
⑧	Afraid and lost, he wanted to drown in the river.	( )
⑨	But when he looked at his reflection in the river,	( )
⑩	he realized that he was not an ugly duckling, but a beautiful swan!	( )

Moral: You are beautiful just the way you are.

LISTEN 2 (Track 4-4)

> **Directions**
>
> Listen to the sentences below. Mark whether you hear the affirmative or the negative. Then, check your answers.

① I (can / can't) make it tomorrow.
② She (can / can't) find the lost child.
③ We (can / can't) finish the report and email it by today.
④ They (are / aren't) allowed to get into the facilities.
⑤ You (were / weren't) pleased to do such a thing.
⑥ I (should / shouldn't) have reported to the boss what was happening.

 LISTEN 3 (Track 4-5)

> **Directions**

1. Listen to the dialog with half of the words missing. Can you understand the dialog? (Track 4-5-1)

Dialog

Waitress: Good morning. _____ _____ ready _____ order?
Customer: Yes, _____ _____ starter, _____ like vegetable soup.
Waitress: _____ what _____ _____ like _____ _____ main course?
Customer: _____ like _____ T-bone steak _____ potatoes.
Waitress: Yes, sir. How _____ _____ like _____ steak?
Customer: Well-done, please.
Waitress: Anything _____ drink?
Customer: Yes, _____ cup _____ coffee, please.
Waitress: Thanks.

2. Now, listen to the complete dialog. Fill in the blanks with the words you hear. Then, check your answers. (Track 4-5-2)
3. Answer the questions in the quiz below. Then, check your answers.

QUIZ

1. What types of words did you have in the blanks? _____
2. Were the words in the blanks stressed or not stressed in the dialog? _____

Answers: 1. function/structure words.   2. Not stressed

💬 SPEAK 1: Ordering Drinks at a Cafe

Directions

1. Analyze the conversation by marking all the stressed words.
2. Mark schwa sounds. Use the example conversation to help you.
3. Get into pairs. Partner A asks questions about ordering drinks and partner B answers. Use the "Drinks" table to help you.
4. Once finished, switch roles.

Example Conversation

Barista: Hi! **WHAT** can I **GET YOU**?
            /ə/
Customer: I'd **LIKE** a **_TALL SKINNY VANILLA NO FOAM LATTE._**
                         /ə/   /ə/   /ə/
Barista: **WHAT'S** your **NAME**?
                      /ə/
Customer: It's **_CLAUDIA_**.
                 /ə/
Barista: **HOW** do you **SPELL** that?
                           /ə/
Customer: **_C-L-A-U-D-I-A_**.

Barista: Is that for **HERE** or to **GO**?
                        /ə/   /ə/
Customer: To **GO**, please.
            /ə/
Barista: That is a **_TALL SKINNY VANILLA NO FOAM LATTE_**. That will be **_5,600 won_**.
                     /ə/   /ə/   /ə/
Customer: Can I **PAY** by **CARD**?
            /ə/

Barista: YES, for SURE.
                      /ə/
Customer: THANK you.

Dialog

Barista: Hi! What can I get you?

Customer: I'd like a *(size & shot/ milk/ syrup/ additional/ drink)*.

Barista: What's your name?

Customer: It's _____.

Barista: How do you spell that?

Customer: _____.

Barista: Is that for here or to go?

Customer: _____, please.

Barista: That is a *(size & shot/ milk/ syrup/ additional / drink)*. That will be _____.

Customer: Can I pay by card?

Barista: Yes, for sure.

Customer: Thank you.

Drinks

Size & Shots	Milk	Syrup	Additional	Drink
Short – 1 shot	Full fat	Vanilla	Extra hot	Latte
Tall – 1 shot	Skimmed	Caramel	Extra/No foam	Cappuccino
Grande – 2 shots	Skinny	Hazelnut	Whip cream	Mocha
Venti – 3 shots	Soy			Caramel Macchiato
				Frappuccino
(Extra shot)				Green tea
				English breakfast

66   SOUNDS CLEAR

SPEAK 2: Team Project (Worksheet, pp. 195-198)

Directions

Suppose you have a pair/team project to complete, and you need to schedule in some time to work on your project. Talk together and find a suitable time.

1. Work in pairs or teams of 4.
2. Take roles asking and answering questions about when you are free, using the timetables provided. Use the example conversation to help you.
3. Pay close attention to the stressed content words and the unstressed function words.
4. Once finished, switch roles.

Questions

- When's your busiest day?
- When's your easiest day?
- What time do you eat lunch?
- Where do you eat lunch?
- When are you free?
- Are you free in the afternoon?
- Are you free in the morning?
- At what time are you free?

Example Conversation

Student 1: When are you free this week?

Student 2: I'm free on *Thursday* at *ten* and *Sunday* at *four*.

Student 1: Great, I'm free at those times, too!

Student 2: Which day would you prefer?

Student 1: I think I'd prefer *Thursday*.

Student 2: Awesome. See you on *Thursday* at *ten*.

Chapter 5
PHRASING AND LINKING

 BACKGROUND INFORMATION

Q. What is phrasing?

A. In conversation, speakers do not say long sentences once in one breath. Instead, they divide them into smaller groups of words that form grammatically coherent units that express an idea. Phrasing is a process of dividing speech into meaningful groups of words. These groups of words are called various names such as "thought groups", "meaning groups", "rhythm groups", "intonation groups", "breath groups", and so on. In this textbook, we will refer to them as thought groups. In written English, punctuation marks such as commas and periods are used to indicate thought groups. However, in spoken English, thought groups are marked with a short break, namely a pause.

Q. Why is phrasing important?

A. Phrasing has beneficial impacts on intelligibility. Speakers divide their speech into thought groups to make the meaning clear. Thought groups also help listeners better understand the information in the speakers' speech by organizing it into comprehensible chunks that are easy to process. Also, when an utterance is phrased differently, it can change the meaning of the utterance.

🎧 Listen to the sentences below. (Track 5-1)

The boss said, "The secretary was hard-working."
"The boss", said the secretary, "was hard-working".

The first sentence where a pause is placed after *The boss said*, means *The secretary was hard-working*. On the other hand, the second sentence with a pause after *The boss* and before *was hard-working* means *The boss was hard-working*. Changing the place of a pause in an utterance can result in a difference in meaning.

Q. How often should speakers pause when they speak?

A. There are no strict rules for how long each thought group should be or how often speakers should pause. Pausing may differ from speaker to speaker, depending on the meaning and the situation. For instance, in informal conversations or slow speeches, thought groups may be shorter, and pauses between the groups may be more frequent than formal speeches or long speeches.

Q. Are some words within a thought group said as if they are one word?

A. Yes, they are. In English, words which are within the same thought group are linked together as if they are one word.

🎧 Listen to the words below. (Track 5-2)

stop pushing	(sounds like sto-/p:/ushing)
roll up	(sounds like ro-/l:/up)
no owl	(sounds like no-/w/owl)

PRACTICE ACTIVITIES

 LISTEN 1 (Track 5-3)

Directions

Listen to the sentences. Put a double slash (⫽) where the speaker pauses between thought groups. Then, check your answers.

Ex. She completed her assignments ⫽ very late at night.

① You should take your car in for service.
② I did not know there was milk in the refrigerator.
③ Their bike moves way faster than your bike does.
④ Customers buy less products whenever the price goes up.
⑤ I was snappy with him because I was running late for work.

 LISTEN 2 (Track 5-4)

Directions

Listen to the sentences and questions below, and mark the appropriate responses. Then, check your answers.

① ☐ a. The class has tests that are two hours long.
   ☐ b. The class has two tests that are an hour long each.

② ☐ a. It is the teacher who is late.
   ☐ b. It is the student who is late.

③ ☐ a. What kind of fruit did they buy?
   ☐ b. They only bought cake and pies.

PHRASING AND LINKING 71

④ ☐ a. Thank you for introducing her to me.
  ☐ b. Your wife has a lovely name.

⑤ ☐ a. (A + B) x C = Y
  ☐ b. A + (B x C) = Y

 LISTEN 3 (Track 5-5)

Directions

Listen to the phrases below. Mark *Same*, if the phrases in each pair sound the same. Mark *Different*, if the phrases in each pair sound different. Then, check your answers.

			Same	Different
Ex.	let her	letter	☑	☐
①	tall or	taller	☐	☐
②	them all	the mall	☐	☐
③	make up	make cup	☐	☐
④	red eye	red dye	☐	☐
⑤	know all	no wall	☐	☐
⑥	made your league	major league	☐	☐

LISTEN AND SPEAK (Track 5-6)

> **Directions**
>
> **1.** Listen to the passage below. Put a double slash (//) where the speaker pauses between thought groups and put an underline between words that are linked. Then, check your answers.
>
> This evening the ant told my three-year-old daughter that owls were nocturnal. My daughter responded "Yes owls are not turtles."
>
> **2.** Read the passage out loud, putting a pause between thought groups and linking words within thought groups.

Pronunciation Tip

Linking the Same /C/ + /C/

When two identical consonants come together in a thought group, they are said like one long consonant represented with /:/. The following words in the passage in "Listen and Speak" are pronounced as if they are one word.

ol<u>d d</u>aughter	(sounds like ol-/d:/aughter)
an<u>t t</u>old	(sounds like an-/t:/old)
daughte<u>r r</u>esponded	(sounds like daughte-/r:/esponded)
no<u>t t</u>urtles	(sounds like no-/t:/urtles)

Linking /C/ + /V/

When a word ends in a consonant and the following word begins with a vowel, the final consonant is linked to the vowel of the following word. The following words in the passage in "Listen and Speak" are linked as such.

thi<u>s e</u>vening	(sounds like thi-/s/evening)
yea<u>r o</u>ld	(sounds like yea-/r/old)
owl<u>s a</u>re	(sounds like owl-/z/are)

PHRASING AND LINKING

Linking /V/ + /V/

In a thought group where a word ends in a tense vowel or a diphthong and the next word begins with a vowel, the off-glide of the final vowel of the first word connects with the first vowel of the next word, as below.

/y/ glide

/iy/ + V	se<u>e o</u>wls	(sounds like see-/y/owls)
/ɔy/ + V	to<u>y a</u>irplane	(sounds like toy-/y/airplane)
/ay/ + V	bu<u>y o</u>il	(sounds like buy-/y/oil)

/w/ glide

/uw/ + V	kne<u>w a</u>ll	(sounds like kne-/w/all)
/ow/ + V	n<u>o e</u>gg	(sounds like no-/w/egg)
/aw/ + V	ho<u>w i</u>s	(sounds like how-/w/is)

Linking /t, d/ + /y/

When a word ends in /t/ and the next word begins with /y/ in a thought group, the two sounds are blended and pronounced /tʃ/ as in *church*. Similarly, when a word ends in /d/ and the next word begins with /y/, the two sounds are blended and pronounced /dʒ/ as in *judge*.

/t/ + /y/	Don't you know...?	(sounds like don-/tʃ/ou)
	Haven't you heard...?	(sounds like haven-/tʃ/ou)
/d/ + /y/	Did you...?	(sounds like di /dʒ/ou)
	Could you...?	(sounds like coul /dʒ/ou)

SPEAK 1: Worst Day Ever?

> **Directions**

1. Read the poem by Chanie Gorkin[5] below out loud twice. The first time from top to bottom and the second time from bottom to top. Mark all the stressed words. See if you notice any difference between the two versions.

> **Version 1 - Top to Bottom**

Today was the absolute worst day ever
And don't try to convince me that
There's something good in every day
Because, when you take a closer look,
This world is a pretty evil place.
Even if
Some goodness does shine through once in a while
Satisfaction and happiness don't last.
And it's not true that
It's all in the mind and heart
Because
True happiness can be attained
Only if one's surroundings are good.
It's not true that good exists
I'm sure you can agree that
The reality
Creates
My attitude
It's all beyond my control
And you'll never in a million years hear me say that
Today was a very good day

---

5   Gorkin, Chanie. 2014. "Worst Day Ever" in *Poetry Nation*, Retrieved from https://www.poetrynation.com/poems/worst-day-ever/

Version 2 - Bottom to Top

Today was the absolute worst day ever
And don't try to convince me that
There's something good in every day
Because, when you take a closer look,
This world is a pretty evil place.
Even if
Some goodness does shine through once in a while
Satisfaction and happiness don't last.
And it's not true that
It's all in the mind and heart
Because
True happiness can be attained
Only if one's surroundings are good.
It's not true that good exists
I'm sure you can agree that
The reality
Creates
My attitude
It's all beyond my control
And you'll never in a million years hear me say that
Today was a very good day

2. Put a double slash for each thought group and put an underline between words that are linked. Check the example answer.
3. Record yourself saying the poem out loud.

SPEAK 2: Chants & Poems

Directions

1. For each chant/poem, mark all the stressed words.
2. Mark schwa sounds in a different color.
3. Put a double slash for each thought group and put an underline between words that are linked. Check the example answers.

Jack and Jill

Ex. **JACK** ənd **JILL** went_**UP** the **HILL** //

Jack and Jill went up the hill
To fetch a pail of water
Jack fell down and broke his crown
And Jill came tumbling after

Camp Chant - Black Socks

Ex. **BLACK SOCKS** // they **NE**vər get **DIR**ty //

Black socks, they never get dirty
The longer you wear them the stronger they get
Sometimes I think I should wash them
But something inside me says No no not yet

Old Man Named Bob

Ex. thər wəz ən **OLD MAN NAMED BOB** //

There was an old man named Bob who never found joy in his job
He wanted to quit but he couldn't admit that he did love to hear himself sob

SPEAK 3: One Fry, Two Fries

Directions

1. Work in pairs.
2. One of you is the teacher, and one of you is the student. Take turns asking and answering questions about plurals, paying close attention to each thought group, and linked words. Use the target words, compliments, and encouragements from the list and the example conversation to help you.
3. Once finished, switch roles.
4. (Optional) Annotate a script you have written for a presentation. You can use an old script or write a new one. Mark thought groups and linked words.

Target Words

potato chip/fry/fries

sausagy/sausage/sausages

ramyeon/noodle/noodles

-s/-es/-ies

Compliments & Encouragements

You're so close.

Try again.

Terrific!

Keep on trying.

You're almost there.

You can do it.

Example Conversation

Teacher:	Look at the picture. // What do you see? //
Student:	*Potato chip*. //
Teacher:	That's almost right. // These are *fries*. // Let's count them together. // One *fry*, // two *fr* … // Oh, // what is it? // What can I say? //
Students:	*Fries*. //
Teacher:	Brilliant. // One *fry*, // two *fries*, // three *fries*! // How do you spell *fries*? // With s, // es, // ies // , or nothing. //
Students:	*s*! //
Teacher:	*Good try*! // But we spell fries with *ies*. // Let's spell it together 1, 2, 3 … //
Teachers & Students:	*F-r-i-e-s*, // *Fries*! //

Chapter 6

PROMINENCE IN DISCOURSE

BACKGROUND INFORMATION

Q. How is the most important word signified in a thought group in English?

A. The most important word in every thought group, called the focus word in this book, is indicated by emphasizing it more prominently than all other stressed words in the thought group. Therefore, the focus word is easier to hear.

Listen to the dialog below. (Track 6-1)

> John: I **FOUND** my **JAC**ket. //
>
> Mary: **WHICH JAC**ket? //
>
> John: The **JAC**ket with **POL**ka dots, // the one I **LIKE** the **MOST**. //

When a conversation begins, the focus is usually on the stressed syllable of the last content word, for example, *JACket* in the above dialog. Once the conversation has begun, new information in one sentence may become old information in the next sentence. The focus can be changed to emphasize the new or important parts of the information as in **WHICH**, **POLka** and **MOST** in the second and third utterances above. Furthermore, the focus can also be shifted to contrast the old information with the new one, as in the following dialog.

🎧 Listen to the dialog below. (Track 6-2)

John: Did you **SPRAIN** your **AN**kle?
Mary: **NO**, I **SPRAINED** my **WRIST**.

The context of the conversation affects which stressed word in a given thought group receives focus. The following examples show how the focus word depends on the context.

🎧 Listen to the dialog below. (Track 6-3)

Context	Focus
What about Cavin?	He **CAN'T COME** to the **PAR**ty.
Who can't come?	He **CAN'T** COME to the **PAR**ty. (pointing to Cavin)
Why won't Cavin come?	He **CAN'T COME** to the **PAR**ty.

⭐ PRACTICE ACTIVITIES

🎧 LISTEN 1 (Track 6-4)

Directions

Listen to the prompts and mark the responses with the correct focus. Then, check your answers.

  ☐ a. I just got back from the clinic.
    ☐ b. I just got back from the clinic.

  ☐ a. I'll get a bank loan to buy your car.
    ☐ b. I'll get a bank loan to buy your car.

③ ☐ a. Let's get a large mushroom pizza.
    ☐ b. Let's get a large mushroom pizza.

④ ☐ a. She **mailed** it.
☐ b. She **faxed** it.

⑤ ☐ a. Oh, I thought it be**gan** at four-thirty.
☐ b. Oh, I thought it began at **four**-thirty.

⑥ ☐ a. I said **four** times six.
☐ b. I said four **times** six.

⑦ ☐ a. **I** found it.
☐ b. I **found** it.

⑧ ☐ a. I **couldn't** attend it.
☐ b. I couldn't at**tend** it.

LISTEN 2 (Track 6-5)

Directions

Listen to the passage from Kaye (1984, p.8)[6]. Put a dot above the focus word in each thought group. Check the example answer.

Ex. It was **HARD** // to get **LAR**ry // to **CON**centrate on **REA**ding // or anything **EL**se. //

He was a perpetual motion machine // and his mind // was as jittery // as his body. //

The only time // I saw Larry work // with concentrated attention //

was when he modelled little clay figures. //

I started using play dough // to focus his attention on reading. //

We began making letters and words // out of play dough. //

---

6 Peggy Kaye. 1984. *Games for Reading: Playful Ways to Help your Child to Read*. New York: Pantheon Books.

This was a turning point for Larry. //

He couldn't learn // at this stage of his life // by studying with paper and pencil. //

But he could learn // by studying with big wads of play dough. //

 LISTEN AND SPEAK (Track 6-6)

Directions

1. Read the dialog out loud. Put a dot above the focus word in each thought group.

Dialog

Assistant: May I help you? //

Customer: Yes, I'd like to return this top. //

Assistant: Can I ask // why you're returning this? //

Customer: I bought it for my son // but it's too big. //

Assistant: There are no refunds // if the items were on sale. //

Customer: Do you have the top // in a smaller size? //

Assistant: Let me check. //

2. Listen to the dialog. Then, check your answers.
3. ⓐ Work in pairs.
   ⓑ Take roles and have a dialog. Put a pause between thought groups and highlight the focus word as well.
   ⓒ Once finished, switch roles.

SPEAK 1: The Danger of a Single Story

Directions

1. Record yourself reading the passage by Chimamanda Ngozi Adichie[7] below.

I'm a storyteller and I would like to tell you a few personal stories about what I like to call the danger of the single story I grew up on a university campus in eastern Nigeria my mother says that I started reading at the age of two although I think four is probably close to the truth so I was an early reader and what I read were British and American children's books I was also an early writer and when I began to write at about the age of seven stories in pencil with crayon illustrations that my poor mother was obligated to read I wrote exactly the kinds of stories I was reading all my characters were white and blue-eyed they played in the snow they ate apples and they talked a lot about the weather how lovely it was that the sun had come out now this despite the fact that I lived in Nigeria I had never been outside Nigeria we didn't have snow we ate mangoes and we never talked about the weather because there was no need to.

---

7   Adichie, C. N. 2009. *The danger of a single story* [Video file]. Retrieved from https://www.ted.com/talks/chimamanda_ngozi_adichie_the_danger_of_a_single_story

2. Once finished, record yourself again. This time, before you read, mark the thought groups and the focus word(s). As you read, pay close attention to the pauses between thought groups and emphasize the focus words. Check the example answer.
3. Do you notice any differences between your first and second recording? If so, what do you notice?

 SPEAK 2: Focus Tic Tac Toe (Worksheet, pp. 199-200)

> **Directions**
> 1. Work in pairs.
> 2. Decide who is X and who is O.
> 3. Take turns reading sentences, emphasizing the focus word, and mark X or O on the box.
> 4. Alternate moves, until one player has drawn a row of 3 symbols (in any direction) or until no one can win the game.

SPEAK 3: Eliciting Vocabulary

> **Directions**
>
> *Imagine you are trying to elicit vocabulary from your students.*
>
> 1. Work in pairs.
> 2. Take roles and have a dialog. Put a pause between thought groups and highlight the focus word in each thought group.
> 3. Switch roles.

Dialog

Teacher: This week we will study about illness. // That's when we are sick. // Eddie has a headache. // What can Eddie do to get better? //

Students: Slip //

Teacher: Ah, you mean *sleep*. // That's right. // He should sleep. Let's say it together 3, 2, 1. //

Students: *Sleep* //

Teacher: What else can he do? //

Students: Medicine //

Teacher: Good answer. // We can take medicine. // Repeat after me. // *Take medicine.* //

Students: *Take medicine* //

PROMINENCE IN DISCOURSE

SPEAK 4: Food Debate

Directions

1. Work in pairs. Pick a topic from the debate box below.
2. Partner A can only ask questions using the question box. Partner B can only answer.
3. See how long you can make your partner talk by asking as many questions as possible.
4. Once finished, switch roles.

The Question Box

About reasons for believing
- Why do you think so?
- What's your evidence for that?
- What makes you say that?

About importance
- How is that good/bad?
- How is that important?
- Why does that matter?

When you want more details about a reason
- Can you explain why?
- Can you be more specific?

When you want another reason
- Give me another reason…
- Can you tell me more reasons?

The Debate Box

① Ketchup on fries or on the side?
② Jjajangmyun or Jjamppong?
③ Ice cream on a cone or in a cup?
④ Pasta swirled on a spoon or slurped as you go along?
⑤ Tangsuyuk covered in sauce or sauce on the side?
⑥ Crispy cereal or soggy cereal?
⑦ Fried or yangnyum chicken?
⑧ Ketchup or mayo?
⑨ Edge of the cake or center of the cake?
⑩ Pineapple or no pineapple on pizza?
⑪ Cow milk or soymilk?
⑫ Cheese tteok or plain tteok?
⑬ Do you fold your pizza or eat it flat?
⑭ Dark chocolate or milk chocolate?
⑮ Deep pan pizza or thin crust?
⑯ Chunky jam or smooth jam?
⑰ Hot Americano or iced Americano?
⑱ Cucumber fan or hater?
⑲ Chicken with bone or no bone?
⑳ Who is king? Chicken or pizza?

Chapter 7
INTONATION

BACKGROUND INFORMATION

Q. What is intonation, and why is it important in speech?

A. The notes of voice are called pitch, or tone. When you speak, your voice rises and falls, and this change in pitch is referred to as intonation. Different pitches may indicate different meanings and emotions for the same utterance. For example, the word *really* can express different meanings and emotions, depending on the pitch you use. A falling tone signifies a statement while a rising tone indicates a question. Also, a falling tone indicates disbelief, a rising tone shows surprise, and a flat tone, or no change in tone, can sound sarcastic. Intonation makes speech meaningful. If you don't use the right pitch, you may not be well understood even when you use the right words and grammar.

Q. What are the major intonation patterns in English?

A. English has two basic intonation patterns, falling and rising. In falling intonation, the pitch goes down from the last stressed syllable in an utterance, called tonic syllable. Falling intonation is also called rise-fall intonation since before the pitch of voice goes down, it rises on the vowel sound of the last stressed word in a thought group. In contrast, in rising intonation, pitch goes up from the last stressed syllable in an utterance and continues to rise to the end.

Listen to the statement and question below. (Track 7-1)

	Statement		Question
High	seen		seen it?
Medium	You've	Have you	
Low		it.	

The statement starts on the medium tone, rises to the high tone on *seen* and falls to the low tone on *it*. On the other hand, the question begins on the medium tone, rises to the high tone on *seen* and continues to rise to the end.

In falling intonation, pitch falls to the low tone in two ways, glide and step. If the last stressed syllable is not followed by any unstressed syllables in a thought group, the tone glides down. In contrast, if the last stressed syllable is followed by any unstressed syllables, the tone steps down.

 Listen to the sentences below. (Track 7-2)

Glide: It smells good.

Step: I'll go on a picnic.

★ PRACTICE ACTIVITIES

🎧 LISTEN 1 (Track 7-3)

Directions

Listen to the utterances, paying close attention to the intonation at the end of the utterances. Circle the letter of the intonation you hear. Then, check your answers.

Ex. I'm not quite sure about his status.   b. ↗

① Do you enjoy living near the seaport?   a. ↘   b. ↗

② How do you like your new job?   a. ↘   b. ↗
③ She'll be back in a minute.   a. ↘   b. ↗
④ What did you say?   a. ↘   b. ↗
⑤ Go see your doctor.   a. ↘   b. ↗
⑥ Is that so?   a. ↘   b. ↗
⑦ She's so kind!   a. ↘   b. ↗
⑧ When do you move to your new house? a. ↘   b. ↗
⑨ You're hungry?   a. ↘   b. ↗
⑩ Really?   a. ↘   b. ↗

Pronunciation Tip

Falling intonation is the most common intonation pattern in English. It is normally used in statements, commands, wh-questions, and exclamations. On the other hand, yes-no questions and statements used to ask a question or to check something uncertain are usually said with rising intonation.

 LISTEN 2 (Track 7-4)

Directions

Listen to the utterances below, paying close attention to the intonation. Mark the rising intonation with an upward arrow (↗) and the falling intonation with a downward arrow (↘) of each intonation group in the square. Then, check your answers.

① He's late this morning ☐, // isn't he ☐? //
② How will you pay ☐, // cash ☐, // or card ☐? //
③ Where are you going for your break ☐, // France ☐, // Italy ☐, // or Sweden ☐? //
④ It's going to rain this afternoon ☐, // isn't it ☐? //
⑤ I'm taking math ☐, // biology ☐, // calculus ☐, // and English ☐. //
⑥ What season do you like the most ☐, // spring ☐, // summer ☐, // fall ☐, // or winter ☐? //

Pronunciation Tip

Tag Question

A tag question is a question added to a statement. When speakers say tag questions with a falling tone, they intend to ask for confirmation or seek agreement. In contrast, speakers normally say tag questions with a rising tone to show uncertainty and to require an answer.

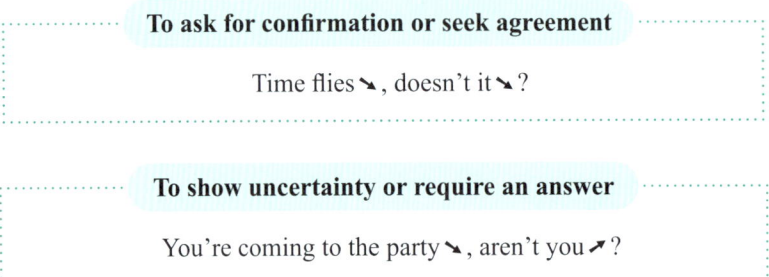

Choice Alternative Question

When choice alternative questions are said with a falling tone at the end, the listener is expected to choose from the closed set of choices being presented. On the other hand, when speakers say choice alternative questions with a rising tone at the end, the listener has a free choice of the alternatives with the chance to turn down all the alternatives being presented.

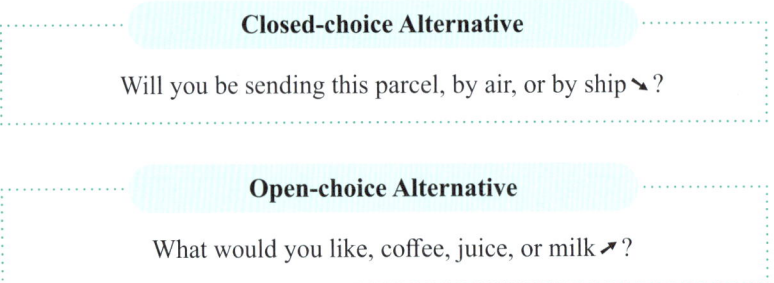

Series Intonation

When speakers list items, they use a rising tone on the items except for the last item. For the last item, a falling tone is normally used.

> **Series Intonation**
>
> I want to buy some apples ↗, bananas ↗ and grapes ↘.

 LISTEN AND SPEAK (Track 7-5)

Directions

1. In the dialog, mark the rising intonation with an upward arrow (↗) and the falling intonation with a downward arrow (↘) of each thought group.

Dialog

A: Do you have the time ☐? //

B: Yes, I do ☐. // It's already 5:30 ☐. //

A: Are you coming home ☐ // or going to the office ☐? //

B: I'm going to the office ☐. //

A: What are your plans for this weekend ☐? //

B: I don't know ☐. // Do you want to get together ☐ // or something ☐? //

A: How about eating out for dinner ☐? //

B: That sounds like a good idea ☐. // Where do you want to meet ☐? //

A: Let's meet at Tafach Doro ☐. //

B: Great ☐! // I heard they just came up with a new pizza ☐ // pasta ☐ // and dessert ☐. //

A: It should be good ☐ // because they always have the best food in town ☐. //

2. Listen to the dialog and check your answers.
3. Work in pairs. Take roles and have a conversation, paying close attention to the intonation of each thought group. Then, switch roles.

INTONATION

SPEAK 1: Asking Questions

> **Directions**
>
> 1. In the dialog below, mark thought groups, the focus word(s), and intonation, as shown in the example. Then, check the example answer.
> 2. Work in pairs.
> 3. Take roles to say the dialog. One of you will be the teacher giving instructions, and the other will be the student.
> 4. Once finished, switch roles and repeat the dialog.

Example

Teacher 1: Look at this picture! ↘ // What's different about these buses? ↘ //

Are these buses the same? ↗ //

Dialog

Teacher: Look at this picture!

What's different about these buses?

Are these buses the same?

Students: No.

Teacher: That's right. These buses have different colors.

Do you know 'Tayo'?

Let's learn colors with a fun Tayo song. (*Demonstrate singing*)

Let's sing together! (*Sing with students*)

[Repeat the song with different colors; blue, green, yellow, and pink.]

Tayo Color Song

 There were cars in the bed, and the little one said, "Roll over, roll over". So, they all rolled over and one fell out, <u>red, red</u>!

Teacher: Awesome job!

SPEAK 2: Lesson Introduction

Directions

1. Mark the intonation of each thought group in the dialog below, introducing different lessons. Then, check the example answers.

Dialog

Teacher 1:	Hello, everyone ☐. // My name is Ryan ☐. // I'm cool ☐, // right ☐? //
Teacher 2:	I'm Rachel ☐, // and I'm kind ☐. //
Teacher 3:	And I'm Reese ☐. // I'm handsome ☐, // aren't I ☐? //
All Teachers:	We're your English teachers ☐ // today ☐. //
Teacher 1:	(student name) ☐ // (Question 1) ☐. //
Student:	(answer) ☐. //
Teacher 2:	Great! (Question 2) ☐. //
Student(s):	(answer) ☐. //
Teacher 3:	That's right ☐. // Today's topic is ☐ // (Topic) ☐. // We are going to learn about ☐ (Objective) ☐ // and later we will speak with friends about it ☐. //
All Teachers:	Are you ready ☐? //

Lesson	Question 1	Question 2	Topic	Objective
1	What did you eat today?	If I want to cook, where can I go?	I'm in the kitchen.	the names of the rooms in a house.
2	What's in here? (showing a pencil case)	What's this? (showing a pencil)	Do you have a pencil?	the names of school objects like pencil, pen, ruler…
3	Can you guess what this is? (showing a thumb up)	Do you know what this red fruit is? (showing a picture of an apple)	Do you like apples?	the food we like and don't like.
4	How's the weather today?	Can we play outside?	It's snowing.	the weather.

2. Work in groups of 4. Take roles introducing an English lesson. Three of you will be the teachers and one of you will be the student.
3. Have a dialog. Use the questions, topics and objectives provided to help you.
4. Once finished, switch roles and repeat the dialog.

SPEAK 3: Intonation Bingo (Worksheet, pp. 201-202)

Directions

1. Work in pairs or groups of 3 or 4.
2. Roll the dice to determine the emotion. The 1st roll determines the column and the 2nd roll determines the row in the Emotion Table.
3. Choose any sentence in the Intonation Bingo and say it according to the emotion and cross it out.
4. If you have crossed out four boxes in any direction in the Intonation Bingo Box, you have one bingo.
5. The first player to get three bingos wins.

SPEAK 4: The Finish Line (Worksheet, p. 203)

Directions

1. Work in pairs or small groups. Decide roles.
2. Roll the dice to determine the column.
3. Read the first sentence in that column with the correct intonation and cross it out.
4. If a player doesn't read the sentence with the correct intonation, they cannot cross it out. They miss a turn.
5. Alternate turns reading sentences until one player reaches the finish line.
6. The player who reaches the finish line first is the winner.

Chapter 8

CONSONANTS

BACKGROUND INFORMATION

Q. How are speech sounds made?

A. When you breathe out, the airstream moves from the lungs into the larynx, the pharynx, and the the oral and nasal cavities. Most speech sounds are made with outward-moving air. Inside the larynx, there are two tiny muscles called the vocal cords. The vocal cords are movable, and they can come close together or be separated apart. The air passages above the larynx are called the vocal tract.

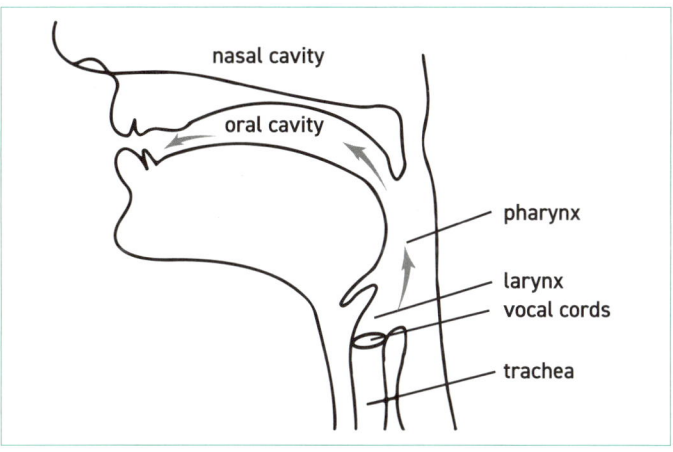

[The Vocal Tract]

All speech sounds are made somewhere in the vocal tract. The vocal organs used to make speech sounds, called articulators, alter the shape of the airstream, as it passes through the oral and nasal cavities, producing different speech sounds.

Q. **Which vocal organs are used to produce sounds in English?**

A. The articulators used to make English sounds are shown below.

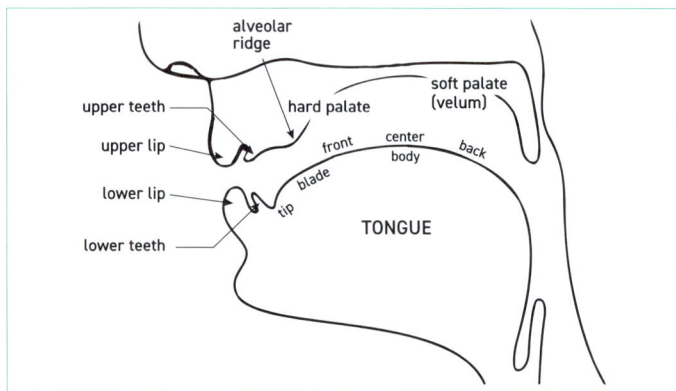

[Articulators for English Sounds]

The upper and lower lips are used to produce English sounds such as /p, b/ and the upper and lower teeth to produce sounds such as /θ, ð/.

On the lower surface of the vocal tract is the tongue. The tongue is divided into the tip, the blade, and the body. The tongue blade is the part right behind the tongue tip. The body part consists of the front, center, and back of the tongue. The tongue part lying right beneath the hard palate is the tongue front, the part that lies beneath the velum is the tongue back, and the part that lies partly beneath the hard palate and partly beneath the soft palate is the tongue center.

In the upper surface of the vocal tract, there is a bony ridge right behind the upper front teeth called the alveolar ridge. The tongue tip and blade are raised against the alveolar ridge to make English sounds such as /t, d, s, z, n, l, r/.

If you place your tongue tip against the alveolar ridge and move your tongue along the mouth's roof, you will feel that the palate becomes increasingly softer. The roof of the mouth, called the palate, is divided into two parts. The front bony part of the palate is called the hard palate and the back soft part is called the soft palate, or the velum. Some sounds in English such as /ʃ, dʒ, y/ are made with the tongue blade or front raised toward the hard palate while some are made with the tongue back raised against the velum /k, g, w/.

Q. What are the classifying criteria of English consonants?

A. English consonants are divided in terms of the states of the glottis and the place and manner of articulation.

States of the Glottis (Voicing)

As mentioned above, the vocal cords are movable. When they are separated apart, the airstream from the lungs flows freely out of the opening between the vocal cords called the glottis, and the vocal cords do not vibrate. On the other hand, if they are close together, the airstream beneath this closure sets the vocal cords in vibration.

[Vocal Cords in Open Position]   [Vocal Cords in Closed Position]

Some sounds are produced without the vocal cords vibrating while others are said with vocal cord vibration. For example, say /z/ with your fingers on your throat or cheeks, and you will feel your vocal cords vibrate. On the other hand, if you say /s/, you will feel no vocal cord vibration. Sounds made with the vocal cord vibration are voiced, and those made without it are voiceless. Although all the vowel sounds in English are voiced, some consonants are voiced and others are voiceless, as illustrated below.

Voiceless	p			t		k		
Voiced	b			d		g		
Voiceless		f	θ	s	ʃ			h
Voiced		v	ð	z	ʒ			
Voiceless					tʃ			
Voiced					dʒ			
Voiced	m			n		ŋ		
Voiced				l, r				
Voiced					y		w	

[Classification of English Consonants in Voicing]

The consonant pairs in each cell are the same in the place and manner of articulation, but they differ in voicing. For example, the consonant sounds /p, b/ only differ in voicing, /p/ being voiceless and /b/ being voiced, while they are the same in the place and manner of articulation, as will be discussed below.

Place of Articulation (Where)

Most consonant sounds in English are made with the complete or partial obstruction of the airstream somewhere in the vocal tract. The point where the airflow is obstructed, completely or partially, is called the place of articulation. English consonants are divided into bilabial, labiodental, interdental, alveolar, palatal, velar, labiovelar, and glottal sounds in terms of the place of articulation.

Place	Description	Consonants	Sagittal Diagram
Bilabial	• Bring the upper and lower lips close together	/p, b, m/	/p, b/
Labiodental	• Raise the lower lip against the upper front teeth	/f, v/	/f, v/
Interdental	• Place the tongue tip between the upper and lower teeth	/θ, ð/	/θ, ð/
Alveolar	• Raise the tongue tip or blade against or near the alveolar ridge	/t, d, s, z, n, l, r/	/t, d/

Palatal	• Raise the tongue blade or front toward the hard palate	/ʃ, ʒ, ʧ, ʤ, y/	/ʃ, ʒ/
Velar	• Raise the tongue back toward the velum	/k, g, ŋ/	/k, g/
Labiovelar	• Raise the tongue back toward the velum, simultaneously rounding the lips	/w/	/w/
Glottal	• Made at the glottis	/h/	/h/

Manner of Articulation (How)

The description of English consonants in terms of the manner of articulation means how the articulators involved come close or how far apart they separate. According to the manner of articulation, English consonants are divided into stop (or plosive), nasal, fricative, affricate, liquid, and glide sounds.

Manner	Description	Consonants	Sagittal Diagram
Stop (Plosive)	• Bring the articulators involved completely together, stopping the air in the mouth • Raise the velum, blocking the air from flowing into the nose • Release the air in the mouth abruptly	/p, b, t, d, k, g/	/t, d/
Nasal	• Bring the articulators involved completely together, stopping the air in the mouth • Lower the velum, allowing the air to flow into the nose • Release the air in the mouth abruptly	/m, n, ŋ/	/n/
Fricative	• Bring the articulators involved approximately close enough to cause air friction • Release the air	/f, v, θ, ð, s, z, ʃ, ʒ, h/	/s, z/
Affricate	• Approximate the articulators involved completely, blocking the air in the mouth • Separate the articulators slightly enough to cause air friction • Release the air	/tʃ, dʒ/	/t, d/ ⇨ /ʃ, ʒ/
Liquid	• Approximate the articulators close to each other, but not to the extent to either stop the airflow or cause friction	/l, r/	/l/ /r/

100 SOUNDS CLEAR

| Glide | • Made with a slight closure of the articulators involved | /w, y/ | /w/ /y/ |

The classification of the 24 English consonants in terms of voicing and the place and manner of articulation is shown below.

Manner	Voicing	Place							
		Bilabial	Labio-dental	Inter-dental	Alveolar	Palatal	Velar	Labio-velar	Glottal
Stop (Plosive)	Voiceless	p			t		k		
	Voiced	b			d		g		
Fricative	Voiceless		f	θ	s	ʃ			h
	Voiced		v	ð	z	ʒ			
Affricate	Voiceless					tʃ			
	Voiced					dʒ			
Nasal	Voiced	m			n		ŋ		
Liquid	Voiced				l, r				
Glide	Voiced					y		w	

[Classification of English Consonants]

🎧 Listen to the 24 English consonant sounds in isolation and in the words below. (Track 8-1)

Consonant	Word	Consonant	Word
/p/	**p**ie	/ð/	**th**y
/b/	**b**ye	/s/	**s**eal
/t/	**t**ime	/z/	**z**eal
/d/	**d**ime	/ʃ/	me**sh**
/k/	**K**ate	/ʒ/	mea**s**ure
/g/	**g**ate	/h/	**h**ire
/m/	**m**at	/tʃ/	**ch**in
/n/	**gn**at	/dʒ/	**j**in
/ŋ/	ga**ng**	/l/	**l**ie
/f/	**f**an	/r/	**r**ye
/v/	**v**an	/w/	**w**et
/θ/	**th**igh	/y/	**y**et

Voiceless vs. Voiced Consonants in English

🎧 Listen to the voiceless and voiced sounds below. (Track 8-2)

/p/, /t/, /k/, /f/, /θ/, /s/, /ʃ/, /tʃ/
/b/, /d/, /g/, /v/, /ð/, /z/, /ʒ/, /dʒ/

Pronunciation Tip

Nasals, liquids, and glides are all voiced in English and Korean. However, stops, fricatives, and affricates in English are divided into voiceless and voiced consonants. On the other hand, in Korean, stops, fricatives, and affricates are all voiceless. The three types of consonants in Korean are classified according to the amount of airflow burst and the degree of vocal cord tenstion: Stops, fricatives, and affricates in Korean are divided into those with a heavy burst of airflow (aspirated), those with a light burst of airflow (unaspirate), those with vocal cord tension (tensed), and those without vocal cord tension (untensed).

	Aspirated, Untensed	Unaspirated, Untensed	Unaspirated, Tensed
Stop	/pʰ, tʰ, kʰ/ (ㅍ, ㅌ, ㅋ)	/p, t, k/ (ㅂ, ㄷ, ㄱ)	/p', t', k'/ (ㅃ, ㄸ, ㄲ)
Fricative		/s/ (ㅅ)	/s'/ (ㅆ)
Affricate	/tʃʰ/ (ㅊ)	/tʃ/ (ㅈ)	/tʃ'/ (ㅉ)

Many Korean-speaking English learners replace English voiced stops, fricatives, and affricates with Korean unaspirated untensed consonants or unaspirated tensed consonants, especially when the voiced stops, fricatives, and affricates come at the beginning of words. When they say voiced stops, fricatives, and affricates in English, they need to make sure that they say them with vocal cord vibration.

PRACTICE ACTIVITIES

LISTEN 1 (Track 8-3)

Directions

Listen and circle the word you hear. Then, check your answers.

Ex. a. rate   (b. raid)

① a. pig   b. big   ② a. dear   b. tear
③ a. cold   b. gold   ④ a. fast   b. vast
⑤ a. either   b. ether   ⑥ a. zip   b. sip
⑦ a. cheap   b. jeep

Pronunciation Rule

Listen to the words ending in voiceless and voiced consonants. Pay close attention to the length of the vowels in the words. (Track 8-4)

① a. rib   b. rip   ② a. laid   b. late
③ a. bag   b. back   ④ a. save   b. safe
⑤ a. teethe   b. teeth   ⑥ a. rice   b. rise
⑦ a. lunch   b. lunge   ⑧ a. batch   b. badge

Rule

The vowels before voiced word-final consonants are _____ than those before voiceless ones.

Answers: longer

Listen to the plural and past tense forms of the words ending in voiceless and voiced consonants. This time, pay close attention to the plural and past tense forms of the words. (Track 8-5)

Plural Forms of Nouns

① a. cats b. lids
② a. lips b. cabs
③ a. cakes b. bags
④ a. chefs b. calves
⑤ a. paths b. lambs

Past Tense Forms of Verbs

① a. wiped b. rubbed
② a. marked b. begged
③ a. roofed b. arrived
④ a. fixed b. raised
⑤ a. pushed b. repaired

Rule

The plural forms of nouns and the past tense forms of verbs are pronounced _____ if the nouns and verbs end in voiceless consonant sounds. On the other hand, they are pronounced _____ if the nouns and verbs end in voiced consonant sounds.

Answers: voiceless (or /s/ and /t/), voiced (or /z/ and /d/)

/p/ as in *pin* vs. /f/ as in *fin*

 Listen to the /p/ and /f/ sounds below. (Track 8-6)

/p/, /p/, /p/, /p/
/f/, /f/, /f/, /f/

Pronunciation Tip

In Korean, there is no distinction between bilabials and labiodentals because Korean does not have labiodentals such as /f/ and /v/. Many Korean-speaking learners of English confuse English /p/ with /f/ and vice versa. They are likely to perceive and produce /p/ and /f/ as an instance of a single consonant sound.

★ PRACTICE ACTIVITIES

 LISTEN 1 (Track 8-7)

Directions

Listen and circle the odd one out. Then, check your answers.

① a. b. c.
② a. b. c.
③ a. b. c.
④ a. b. c.

 LISTEN 2 (Track 8-8)

Directions

Listen and circle the word you hear. Then, check your answers.

① Look at that big (pin, fin) over there.

② The dealers trade (cheap, chief) items only.

③ The sign says, "No (coughs, cops)."

④ The (cliffs, clips) are not safe.

LISTEN AND SPEAK (Track 8-9)

Directions

1. Listen and circle the word you hear. Then, check your answers. (Track 8-9-1)

① a. peel   b. feel
② a. pans   b. fans
③ a. cups   b. cuffs
④ a. past   b. fast

2. Repeat the words after the speaker, paying close attention to the /p/ and /f/ sounds in the words. (Track 8-9-2)

3. Work in pairs. Partner A says one of the prompts in each pair. Partner B replies with the correct response. Once finished, switch roles.

	Prompts	Responses
①	John, close your eyes and (peel, feel) the fruits.	a. He has to be careful not to cut his fingers. b. He can sort out the fruits without looking.
②	Look at the (pans, fans).	a. They're very useful for cooking. b. They'll keep this room cool.
③	The (cups, cuffs) are very fancy.	a. They're used only in fancy restaurants. b. They look well on shirts of any color.
④	She drove (past, fast).	a. She didn't recognize it. b. She should have slowed down.

SPEAK 1: Classroom Quiz

Directions

Imagine that a quiz is being given out to the class.

QUIZ

Look and Write

Fill in the blanks with the words in the box.

earmuffs, pyjamas, pants, puffer jacket

Ex. This is a <u>scarf</u>.

①

This is a _____.

②

This is a pair of _____.

③

This is a pair of _____.

④

This is a pair of _____.

1. Work in groups of 4.
2. Take roles. One of you will be the teacher, and the rest will be the students. Read the dialog out loud.
3. Once finished, switch roles.

Dialog

Teacher: It's time for the quiz.

All students: Uh!

Teacher: Stop talking and face the front. There are four questions. Look at the pictures and fill in the blanks. When you finish, put your pens down.

Student 1: I don't understand. Could you repeat it again, please?

Teacher: OK, let's do an example together. Look at this picture. What is it?

All students: *A scarf*.

Teacher: Fantastic! Now write the word *scarf*. OK, put your books away and take one sheet and pass them on.

Student 2: I dont't have a sheet of paper.

Teacher: OK, I'll bring one for you.

Student 3: I forgot my pen.

Teacher: Come to the front and pick one up. OK, let's start. (*5 minutes later*) Time's up. Stop writing and eyes to the front.

All students: Uh!

SPEAK 2: Are You Adulting? (Worksheet, p. 205)

Directions

1. Complete the survey by ticking the statements you agree with. If you don't agree or you're not sure, leave a blank space.
2. Once finished, interview two other people with the same survey. Write their answers in *Friend 1* and *Friend 2*. Don't forget to ask follow-up questions.
3. When finished, check your score.

Follow-up Questions

- Why do you think so?
- Can you give me an example?
- How so?

	SCORE
0-5 ticks	**Thank you, bank of mum & dad!** You haven't concluded that you are becoming an adult. You definitely still depend a lot on your mum and dad.
6-10 ticks	**Life is all about having fun. YOLO!** You know the concept of adulting, but you're not ready to accept it yet. You love your college lifestyle, and it's all about socializing.
11-15 ticks	**You're definitely on your way!** You've had your fun and are now ready to get serious about adulting. You're trying new things, but sometimes you go back to your old ways.
16-20 ticks	**You've got it made!** You're killing the adulting game! You're a go-getter and a trendsetter. A lot of people of your age either look up to you or come to you for advice.

/b/ as in *boat* vs. /v/ as in *vote*

 Listen to the /b/ and /v/ sounds below. (Track 8-10)

/b/, /b/, /b/, /b/
/v/, /v/, /v/, /v/

Pronunciation Tip

As mentioned before, Korean has no labiodental consonants such as /f/ and /v/. Many Korean-speaking learners of English confuse English /b/ with /v/ and vice versa, perceiving and producing /b/ and /v/ as an instance of a single consonant sound.

PRACTICE ACTIVITIES

 LISTEN 1 (Track 8-11)

Directions

Listen and circle the odd one out. Then, check your answers.

① a. b. c.
② a. b. c.
③ a. b. c.
④ a. b. c.

 LISTEN 2 (Track 8-12)

Directions

Listen and circle the word you hear. Then, check your answers.

① They have no (bowels, vowels).
② The (ban, van) will discontinue from next year.
③ How do you spell (beer, veer)?
④ She whispered, (rebel, revel).

LISTEN AND SPEAK (Track 8-13)

Directions

1. Listen and circle the word you hear. Then, check your answers. (Track 8-13-1)

①	a. bailed	b. veiled
②	a. base	b. vase
③	a. bowed	b. vowed
④	a. boaters	b. voters

2. Repeat the words after the speaker, paying close attention to the /b/ and /v/ sounds in the words. (Track 8-13-2)
3. Work in pairs. Partner A says one of the prompts in each pair. Partner B replies with the correct response. Once finished, switch roles.

	Prompts	Responses
①	The court did not allow him to be (bailed, veiled).	a. He should be in jail. b. He should take it off before entering the court.
②	The second (base, vase) looks better.	a. That's where the military carry out their operations. b. But it's more expensive.
③	She (bowed, vowed) to the audience.	a. It's common when greeting people. b. She'll keep her promise to the audience.
④	The (boaters, voters) look very pleased.	a. They enjoy sailing a lot. b. They won the election.

CONSONANTS

SPEAK 1: Guess Who (Character Bank, p. 207)

Directions

The aim of the game is to guess your opponent's chosen character.

1. Work in pairs. In secret, choose a character from the character bank. Don't show your partner.
2. Take turns asking and answering yes/no questions to guess who your partner has chosen. You can only ask yes/no questions. Use the word bank and the model conversation to help you.
3. The first person to guess their opponent's character wins.

Word Bank

Unique Features	Face Shape	Other	Skin Tone	Hairstyles
stubble	oval	visor/cap	fair	bangs
beard	round	braces	olive	bun
buckteeth	chiseled/	glasses/	brown	dreadlocks
birthmark	square jaw	sunglasses	dark brown	afro
bushy eyebrows		headphones		mohawk
sideburns		turban		wavy
		hijab		buzzcut
				bold

Model Conversation

A: Are you a man?
B: No. Are you young?
A: Yes. Are you from Barbados?
B: No. Are you fair skinned?
A: Yes. Do you have glasses?
B: Yes. Do you have blue eyes?
A: No. Do you have afro hair?
B: Yes. Are you bold?
A: No. Are you Victory?
B: Yes!

A: Bert   B: Victory

SPEAK 2: Giving Directions (Worksheet, pp. 209-210)

> **Directions**
>
> 1. Work in pairs.
> 2. Take turns asking your partner for directions to the places in the blanks on the worksheet.
> 3. Use the model conversation and the expression bank to help you.
> 4. Once finished, check your answers.

Model Conversation

A: Sorry, how do I get to Victoria Park?
B: It's straight ahead. It's opposite the roundabout, on the left.
A: Sorry, could you say that again, please?
B: It's straight ahead. You'll see it when you get to the roundabout.

Expression Bank

- Excuse me, where's the nearest _____? / Sorry, how do I get to _____?
- Go straight./ It's straight ahead.
- Turn right/ left.
- Next to/ between/ behind/ opposite
- Sorry, could you say that again, please?

/θ/ as in *think* vs. /s/ as in *sink*

 Listen to the /θ/ and /s/ sounds below. (Track 8-14)

/θ/, /θ/, /θ/, /θ/
/s/, /s/, /s/, /s/

> **Pronunciation Tip**
>
> Korean has no interdental consonants such as /θ/ and /ð/. Therefore, Korean-speaking learners of English are likely to confuse English /θ/ with /s/ and vice versa, perceiving and producing /θ/ and /s/ as an instance of a single consonant sound.

★ PRACTICE ACTIVITIES

 LISTEN 1 (Track 8-15)

Directions

Listen and circle the odd one out. Then, check your answers.

① a. b. c.
② a. b. c.
③ a. b. c.
④ a. b. c.

 LISTEN 2 (Track 8-16)

Directions

Listen and circle the word you hear. Then, check your answers.

① It does not (thaw, saw) well.
② That's (unthinkable, unsinkable).
③ Two (thumbs, sums) up.
④ It says, "No (songs, thongs)."

🎧 LISTEN AND SPEAK (Track 8-17)

Directions

1. Listen and circle the word you hear. Then, check your answers. (Track 8-17-1)

①	a. faithless	b. faceless
②	a. thumb	b. sum
③	a. mouth	b. mouse
④	a. tense	b. tenth

2. Repeat the words after the speaker, paying close attention to the /θ/ and /s/ sounds in the words. (Track 8-17-2)
3. Work in pairs. Partner A says one of the prompts in each pair. Partner B replies with the correct response. Once finished, switch roles.

	Prompts	Responses
①	He's a (faithless, faceless) angel.	a. No, he has a strong faith. b. Nobody knows who he is.
②	Wow, that was a large (thumb, sum).	a. That's why she wears XXL gloves. b. Yeah, she is quite the generous type.
③	He has a big (mouth, mouse).	a. Yes, he can't keep a secret. b. He has raised it for several years.
④	He is (tense, tenth).	a. I see. That's why he is nervous. b. Who was the ninth then?

CONSONANTS

SPEAK 1: Tongue Twisters

> **Directions**
>
> 1. Brainstorm words that start with /θ/ and /s/. It is best to use rhyming words.
> 2. Use the questions and examples to help you make your tongue twister.
> 3. Try to answer each question with at least one word that starts with /θ/ or /s/, as shown in the examples.
> 4. Once finished, put all the sentences together and teach your tongue twister to a friend.

Brainstorm

	Questions	Example 1	Example 2
①	Who is the person?	Thelma Smith	Sally mouse
②	What did they do? What happened?	Thought of myths	Mouth seemed sore
③	Where did they do it?	At the sink	At Thimble Thumble's house front door
④	When did it happen?	At 3:06	I think it was quarter-past-four
⑤	Why did it happen?	Because she felt incredibly sick	Because the sun was soon to go
⑥	**Put it all together and teach it to a friend.**	**Thelma Smith thought of myths at the sink at 3:06 because she felt incredibly sick.**	**Sally's mouse's mouth seemed sore at Thimble Thumble's house front door. I think it was quarter-past-four because the sun was soon to go.**

	Questions	Tongue Twister
①	Who is the person?	
②	What did they do?	
③	Where did they do it?	
④	When did it happen?	
⑤	Why did it happen?	
⑥	**Put it all together and teach it to a friend.**	

SPEAK 2: Battleship (Worksheet, pp. 211-212)

> **Directions**
>
> *Find the enemy's ships hidden within their grid to win the game.*
>
> 1. Work in pairs.
> 2. Sit opposite your partner and secretly draw five ships on the *My Ships* grid. Each ship is the size of one square.
> 3. Take turns guessing the location of your partner's ships.
> 4. On the *My Enemy's* grid, mark *H* if you hit a ship or *E* if the box is empty.
> 5. The first player to guess all five ships is the winner.

/ð/ as in *though* vs. /d/ as in *dough*

 Listen to the /ð/ and /d/ sounds below. (Track 8-18)

/ð/, /ð/, /ð/, /ð/
/d/, /d/, /d/, /d/

Pronunciation Tip

As mentioned previously, there are no interdentals such as /θ/ and /ð/ in Korean. Therefore, Korean-speaking learners of English are likely to confuse /ð/ with /d/ and vice versa. They tend to perceive and produce English /ð/ and /d/ as an instance of a single consonant sound.

⭐ PRACTICE ACTIVITIES

 LISTEN 1 (Track 8-19)

Directions

Listen and circle the odd one out. Then, check your answers.

① a. b. c.
② a. b. c.
③ a. b. c.
④ a. b. c.

 LISTEN 2 (Track 8-20)

Directions

Listen and circle the word you hear. Then, check your answers.

① I don't believe them, (Ida, either).
② Bill is taller (Dan, than) Jones.
③ (Ds, These) are no good.
④ They shouted, (side, scythe).

LISTEN AND SPEAK (Track 8-21)

Directions

1. Listen and circle the word you hear. Then, check your answers. (Track 8-21-1)

① a. wordy   b. worthy
② a. load   b. loathe
③ a. header   b. heather
④ a. Dave   b. They've

2. Repeat the words after the speaker, paying close attention to the /ð/ and /d/ sounds in the words. (Track 8-21-2)
3. Work in pairs. Partner A says one of the prompts in each pair. Partner B replies with the correct response. Once finished, switch roles.

	Prompts	Responses
①	They're (wordy, worthy).	a. Yes, they're very talkative. b. Yes, they're very valuable.
②	They (load, loathe) the train with many people.	a. The train can accommodate only 50 people. b. They like taking quiet trains.
③	Look at the (header, heather).	a. It cuts the rice paddies well. b. I like its purple petals.
④	(Dave, They've) just arrived at Time Square.	a. He's here to celebrate New Year's Day. b. They're here to celebrate New Year's Day.

Pronunciation Rule

🎧 Listen to the words below, paying close attention to the /t, d/ sounds in the words. (Track 8-22)

①	a. writer	b. rider	②	a. atom	b. Adam
③	a. rater	b. raider	④	a. greater	b. grader
⑤	a. latter	b. ladder			

Does the speaker pronounce the word pairs the same or different? Some native English speakers, particularly speakers using American and Canadian English, say the alveolar stops /t, d/ in the words above like a fast /d/ sound, which is called the flap /ɾ/.

Rule

The stops /t, d/ are pronounced with the flap /ɾ/ when they come between two _____ and the vowel after the alveolar stop is _____.

Answers: vowels, unstressed

🎧 Listen to the words below, paying close attention to the /t, d/ sounds before /r/ in the words. (Track 8-23)

①	a. train	b. chain	①	a. drain	b. Jane
②	a. trill	b. chill	②	a. drill	b. Jill
③	a. trunk	b. chunk	③	a. drunk	b. junk
④	a. true	b. chew	④	a. drew	b. Jew

Does the speaker pronounce the first consonant sound in each word pair the same or different? Some native English speakers pronounce the sounds /t/ and /d/ before /r/ like the initial sound of the words in (b).

Rule

In English, the sounds /t, d/ change into _____ respectively when they occur right before /r/.

Answer: /tʃ, dʒ/

CONSONANTS 121

SPEAK 1: Whose Is It? (Worksheet, p. 213)

Directions

1. Work in pairs or small groups.
2. Toss a coin. Heads moves one space and tails moves two spaces.
3. Ask the question using *this*, *that*, *these* or *those*. Use the example conversation to help you.
4. If you mispronounce a "*th*" sound (/θ/ or /ð/) or do not use *this*, *that*, *these* or *those* correctly, you must go back to where you were.
5. The first person to finish is the winner.

Example Conversation

A: Whose clothes are these?
B: They're Heather's.

SPEAK 2: Desert Island (Item Box, p. 215)

Directions

Suppose that you are stranded on a desert island. The weather is hot; there are coconut trees and freshwater. You do not know when you will be rescued, and you need to make sure, you survive. What items in the box below would you choose to help you stay alive?

1. Work alone, choose three items (from the item box) you would keep with you, and note down your reasons.
2. Make a pair, compare your lists, and choose only three items.
3. Make a group of four and compare your lists.
4. Your final team list should only have three items.

Expression Bank

Statements	Agreeing	Disagreeing
• I think … • Don't you think … • I feel …	• You're right. • That's a good point.	• Maybe/Perhaps, but … • I'm afraid I don't agree. • Frankly speaking …

Example Conversation

A: I think I would choose <u>a hand saw</u> because <u>I can use it to chop wood</u>.

B: You're right. But I have to have <u>the dog</u> because <u>it can keep me company</u>.

A: Don't you think it will be difficult to <u>feed the dog</u>?

B: That's a good point, but <u>I love dogs</u>.

A: Sorry, but I don't agree with that. I think <u>having a first aid kit</u> is more important.

CONSONANTS

/r/ as in *rent* vs. /l/ as in *lent*

🎧 Listen to the /r/ and /l/ sounds below. (Track 8-24)

/r/, /r/, /r/, /r/
/l/, /l/, /l/, /l/

Pronunciation Tip

In English, there are two liquid sounds, /r/ and /l/. When we say /r/, the lips are a little bit rounded while the tip of the tongue does not touch the roof of the mouth. Some speakers of English say /r/ with the tip of the tongue curled up. Others say it with the back of the tongue pulled back and bunched up without curling the tip.

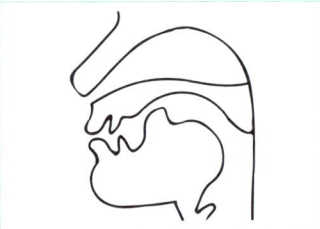
[/r/ with the tongue curled up]

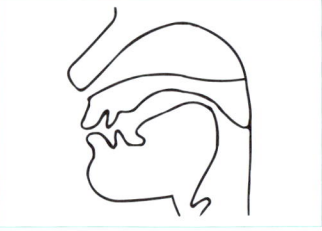
[/r/ with the tongue pulled back]

On the other hand, when we say /l/, the tip of the tongue touches the alveolar ridge, while the sides of the tongue are lowered so air can flow around the lowered tongue. The lips are not rounded when we say /l/ unlike /r/.

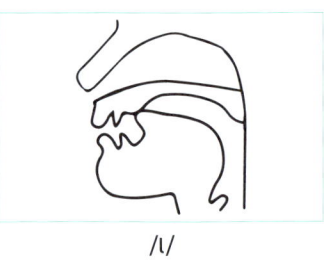
/l/

Many Korean-speaking learners of English confuse English /r/ and /l/ partly due to the influence of their native language in which there is no /r/ and /l/ distinction. So, they are likely to perceive and pronounce /r, l/ as an instance of a single consonant sound.

PRACTICE ACTIVITIES

 LISTEN 1 (Track 8-25)

Directions

Listen and circle the odd one out. Then, check your answers.

① a. b. c.
② a. b. c.
③ a. b. c.
④ a. b. c.

 LISTEN 2 (Track 8-26)

Directions

Listen and circle the word you hear. Then, check your answers.

① We need a bigger (lock, rock).
② The (leaders, readers) were rewarded.
③ That's an interesting (cloud, crowd).
④ (Kneel, Near) to the baby.

LISTEN AND SPEAK (Track 8-27)

Directions

1. Listen and circle the word you hear. (Track 8-27-1)

   ① a. glass   b. grass
   ② a. tool   b. tour
   ③ a. played   b. prayed
   ④ a. flying   b. frying

2. Repeat the words after the speaker, paying close attention to the /r/ and /l/ sounds in the words. (Track 8-27-2)

3. Work in pairs. Partner A says one of the prompts in each pair. Partner B replies with the correct response. Once finished, switch roles.

	Prompts	Responses
①	Look at the green (glass, grass).	a. It was cleaned well. b. It was watered well.
②	That was a marvelous (tool, tour).	a. You can fix many things with it. b. I enjoyed the places we visited so much.
③	They (played, prayed) until it went dark.	a. They had lots of fun. b. They are very faithful.
④	You like (flying, frying), don't you?	a. No, that's why I don't travel overseas. b. No, I don't like greasy foods.

SPEAK 1: The Dial Pad Game (Dial Pad, pp. 217-218)

> **Directions**
>
> 1. Work in pairs.
> 2. Partner A chooses a dial pad and picks a phone number.
> 3. Partner A tells it to partner B by reading out the words on the dial pad. Do not call out the numbers; Only say the words.
> 4. Partner B calls out the numbers. Use the example conversation to help you.
> 5. Once finished, switch roles.

Example Conversation

A: Plus, right, arrive, right, light, really, rental, rally, right, lentil, alive, rental, collect.
B: +353 20 913 8496
A: That's right!

Phone Numbers

Hungary	+36 55 129 142	Congo (Kinshasa)	+243 80 048 5219
Hungary	+36 55 472 601	Congo (Kinshasa)	+243 80 728 9673
Kiribati	+686 41668	Cambodia	+855 09 671 9816
Kiribati	+686 39887	Cambodia	+855 09 851 4252

CONSONANTS 127

SPEAK 2: Lesson Review

Directions

Imagine you are in a classroom reviewing a lesson by playing a game.

1. Work in groups of 3.
2. Take roles, one of you being the teacher and two of you being the students.
3. Read the dialog out loud.
4. Once finished, switch roles.

Dialog

Teacher: Let's play a telepathy game with the words from last class. Can anyone remember the words we learned the last lesson?

Student A: Do you have a pencil?

Teacher: That's right. We asked and answered the question, "Do you have a pencil?" What else did we learn?

Student B: Eraser, ruler, crayon…

Teacher: Brilliant! Let's review the words together.

Teacher & students: Pencil, eraser, ruler, crayon, book and pen.

Teacher: You guys are awesome! Let me tell you the rules of the game.

> First, make groups of 4. Take a board, a marker, and an eraser.
> Second, look at the PPT. There are four pictures. Choose one.
> Third, if you are correct, you win 1 point.
> Fourth, the group with the most points wins.

Let me check your understanding. First, you should make groups of 3, 4 or 5?

All Students: 4.

Teacher: You need an eraser, a marker, and what else?

All Students: A board.

Teacher: The correct answer gets 1 or 2 points?

All students: 1 point.

Teacher: Now, you're ready to play.

/ʒ/ as in *usual* vs. /dʒ/ as in *judge* vs. /z/ as in *zoo*

🎧 Listen to the /ʒ/, /dʒ/ and /z/ sounds below. (Track 8-28)

/ʒ/, /ʒ/, /ʒ/, /ʒ/
/dʒ/, /dʒ/, /dʒ/, /dʒ/
/z/, /z/, /z/, /z/

Pronunciation Tip

English has three distinct consonant sounds /ʒ, dʒ, z/. Firstly, the sounds /ʒ/ and /dʒ/ differ in the manner of articulation, /ʒ/ being a fricative and /dʒ/ being an affricate. Secondly, /ʒ/ is also distinct from /z/ in the place of articulation, /z/ being made at the alveolar ridge and /ʒ/ at the hard palate. Thirdly, /z/ and /dʒ/ differ both in place, /z/ being made at the alveolar ridge and /dʒ/ at the hard palate, and in manner, /z/ being a fricative and /dʒ/ an affricate.

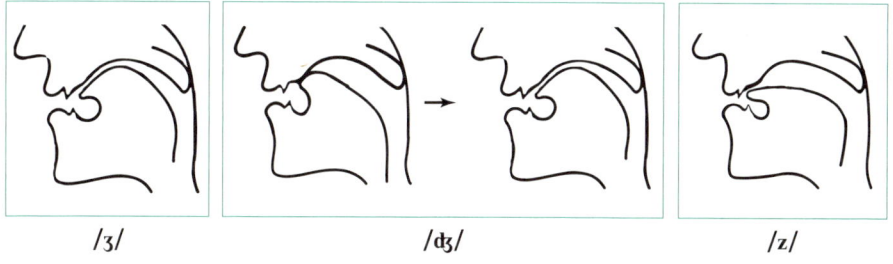

/ʒ/   /dʒ/   /z/

On the other hand, Korean does not make a distinction in these three sounds. So, many Korean-speaking learners of English often err in perceiving and producing them, replacing them all with the Korean consonant /ㅈ/.

PRACTICE ACTIVITIES

 LISTEN 1 (Track 8-29)

Directions

Listen and circle the odd one out. Then, check your answers.

① a. b. c.
② a. b. c.
③ a. b. c.
④ a. b. c.

 LISTEN 2 (Track 8-30)

Directions

Listen and circle the word you hear. Then, check your answers.

① Don't rely on the (pledger, pleasure) too much.
② She says, (ruse, rouge).
③ (Jack, Zach) is popular among his friends.
④ I do not like the (fridge, frizz).

LISTEN AND SPEAK (Track 8-31)

Directions

1. Listen and circle the word you hear. (Track 8-31-1)

① a. legion b. lesion
② a. closure b. closer
③ a. rage b. rays
④ a. Jules b. zoos

2. Repeat the words after the speaker, paying close attention to the /ʒ/, /dʒ/ and /z/ sounds in the words. (Track 8-31-2)

3. Work in pairs. Partner A says one of the prompts in each pair. Partner B replies with the correct response. Once finished, switch roles.

	Prompts	Responses
①	Don't be disturbed by the (legion, lesion).	a. The troops will not invade your area. b. The injury is not serious.
②	You need to get (closure, closer).	a. You'll feel much better afterwards. b. You should move your chair forward.
③	Her note to him was full of (rage, rays).	a. Yes, he made her really angry. b. Yes, she really loves him.
④	The (Jules, zoos) are popular among children.	a. They're a welcoming family. b. There are many cute animals.

SPEAK 1: Dots and Boxes (Worksheet, p. 219)

> **Directions**
>
> *The aim of the game is to complete more boxes than your partner.*
>
> 1. Work in pairs.
> 2. Take turns drawing horizontal or vertical lines from one dot to another. Make a sentence with a word on either side of the line you drew. See examples 1-7 below.
> 3. If you complete the fourth side of a box on your turn, write the first letter of your name in the box. See example 8.
> 4. In addition, you get an extra turn to either draw a line or complete a box.
> 5. Once all of the boxes have been completed, count to see who got the most boxes. See example 9.

EXAMPLES

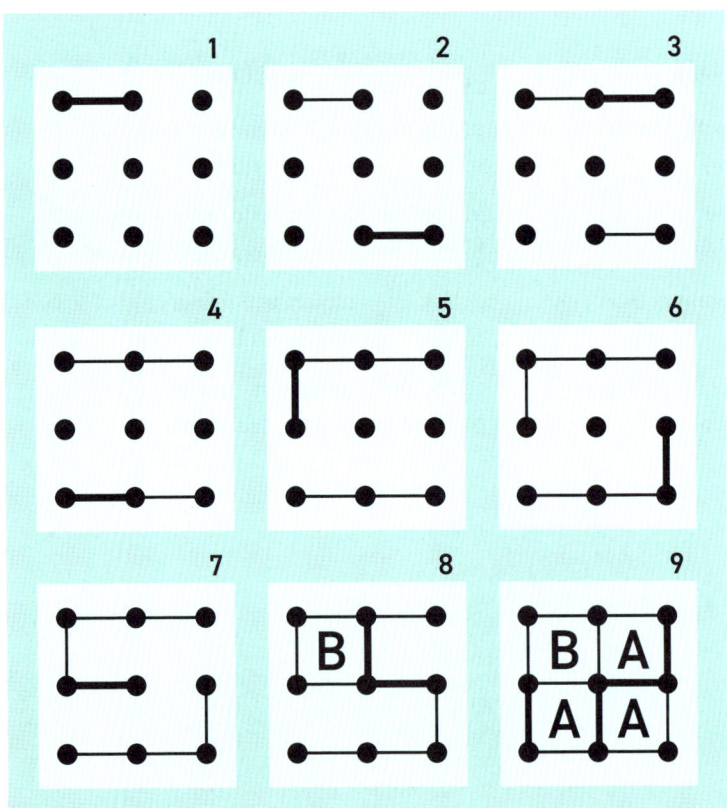

SPEAK 2: The Time Capsule

> **Directions**
>
> 1. Make a time capsule that will be opened 100 years from now.
> 2. First, work alone and choose ten items that are important to you.
> 3. Then, compare your list with a friend and make a pair list. You should only have ten items.
> 4. Get into groups of 4-5 people and make a group list.
> 5. Your final team list should only have ten items altogether.
> 6. You must only choose items that have /ʒ/, /dʒ/, or /z/ sounds.

Your List	Pair List	Group List
1.	1.	1.
2.	2.	2.
3.	3.	3.
4.	4.	4.
5.	5.	5.
6.	6.	6.
7.	7.	7.
8.	8.	8.
9.	9.	9.
10.	10.	10.

/ ʒ / sound	/ dʒ / sounds	/ z / sounds
A television	Your college jacket	A magazine
A collage of your favorite celebrity	Your favorite drink	A razor
Measuring tape	A page from your favorite book	A puzzle
Massage oil	Pajamas	Cookies
A map of Asia	Jeans	A xylophone
Parents Day carnation corsage	An image of your crush	A newspaper
Something you treasure	Your college journal	Dress shoes
Something rouge	Postage stamps	Glasses
A camouflage uniform	Jellybeans	Sheet music of your favorite song
A neck massager	Your favorite bible passages	Your favorite desert recipe
	Juggle balls	

Chapter 9

VOWELS

BACKGROUND INFORMATION

Q. How are English vowels classified?

A. English vowels can be classified in terms of tongue position (advancement and height), muscle tension, and lip position.

Tongue Advancement

According to the tongue position, English vowels can be described in terms of the part of the tongue involved in the production of the sound and the height of the tongue. As for the part of the tongue, the front part of the tongue is pushed forward for the vowels /iy/ as in *beat*, /ɪ/ as in *bit*, /ey/ as in *bait*, /ɛ/ as in *bet*, and /æ/ as in *bat*. These vowels are called front vowels. For vowels /uw/ as in *boot*, /ʊ/ as in *book*, /ow/ as in *boat*, and /ɔ/ as in *bought*, and /ɑ/ as in *bot*, the back part of the tongue is pulled backward. These vowels are back vowels. The vowel /ʌ/ as in *butt* is pronounced with the tongue neither advanced nor retracted, and thus it is classified as a central vowel.

Tongue Height

Regarding the tongue height, some vowels are said with the tongue raised or lowered while others are said with the tongue neither raised nor lowered. Say the front vowels /iy, ɪ, ey, ɛ, æ/ and the back vowels /uw, ʊ, ow, ɔ, ɑ/ in sequence. As you say the front and back vowels in a series, your tongue becomes increasingly lowered. For example, when you say /iy, ɪ, uw, ʊ/, the tongue is raised high, when you say /ey, ɛ, ʌ, ow, ɔ/, the tongue is midway, and when you say /æ, ɑ/, the tongue gets lowered. In English, /iy, ɪ, uw, ʊ/ are high vowels, /ey, ɛ, ʌ, ow, ɔ/ are mid vowels, and /æ, ɑ/ are low vowels.

Muscle Tension

Some vowels are articulated with tensed muscles while others are said with relaxed muscles. Vowels produced with tensed muscles are tense vowels, and vowels with relaxed muscles are lax vowels. The tense vowels /iy, ey, uw, ow/ are glided and longer and said at more peripheral areas in the mouth. On the other hand, the lax vowels /ɪ, ɛ, æ, ʌ, ɑ, ʊ, ɔ/ are not glided and are shorter and are said at the centered areas.

Lip Position

In English, high and mid back vowels /uw, ʊ, ow, ɔ/ are said with the lips pushed out and rounded. These vowels are round. All other vowels /iy, ɪ, ey, ɛ, æ, ʌ, ɑ/ are said with the spread or neutral lips, and these vowels are unround.

The vowels with no change in vowel quality are called monophthongs. The 11 monophthongs we have described can be classified as below.

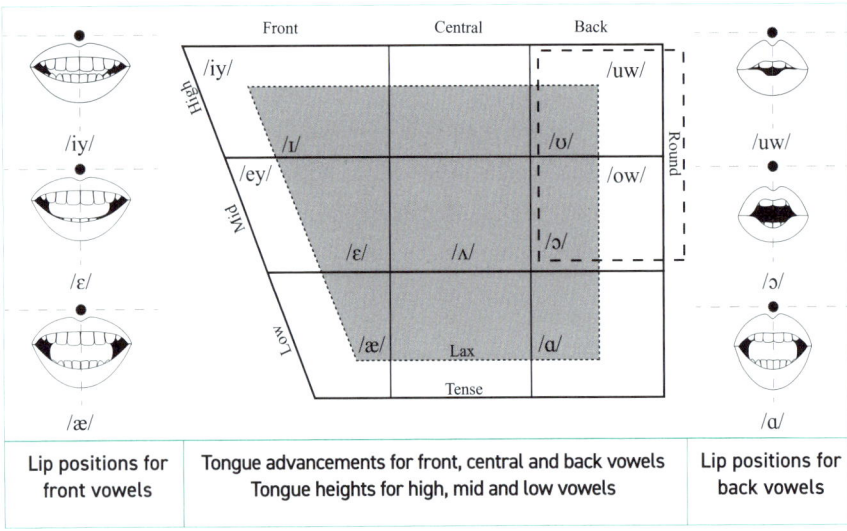

[Classification of English Monophthongs]

Diphthongs

English has three vowels /ay, aw, ɔy/ as in *buy, bow,* and *boy* in which there are noticeable changes in vowel quality. These vowels begin with either the back, low vowel /ɑ/ or the back, mid, lax vowel /ɔ/ and are glided with either /y/ or /w/. These vowels are called diphthongs.

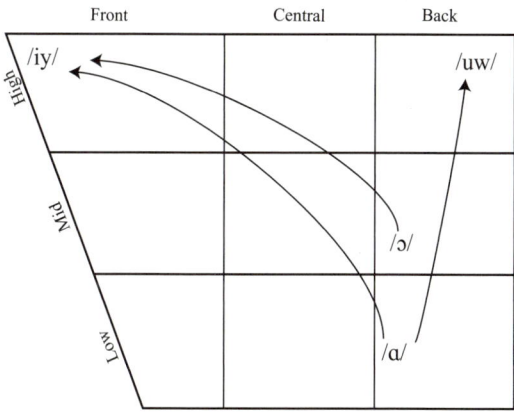

[Classification of English Diphthongs]

Different English speakers have different vowels. The diagrams provided above for the English vowels are intended to provide general guidelines for American English, especially on the location of the vowels during speech.

Listen to the 14 English vowels in isolation and in the words. (Track 9-1)

Vowels	Words	Vowels	Words
/iy/	beat	/uw/	boot
/ɪ/	bit	/ʊ/	book
/ey/	bait	/ow/	boat
/ɛ/	bet	/ɔ/	bought
/æ/	bat	/ay/	buy
/ʌ/	butt	/aw/	bow
/ɑ/	bot	/ɔy/	boy

/iy/ as in *leap* vs. /ɪ/ as in *lip*

🎧 Listen to the /iy/ and /ɪ/ sounds below. (Track 9-2)

/iy/, /iy/, /iy/, /iy/
/ɪ/, /ɪ/, /ɪ/, /ɪ/

/iy/

- Raise the front part of the tongue high, close to the roof of the mouth.
- Spread the lips.
- As you say /iy/, glide the front part of the tongue forward and upward and spread the lips a little more.
- Tense the muscles.

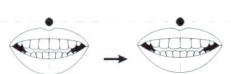
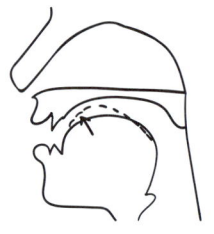

/ɪ/

- Raise the front part of the tongue high, but lower than for /iy/.
- Spread the lips, but less spread than /iy/.
- The tongue and the lips do not glide.
- Say /ɪ/ short.
- Relax the muscles.

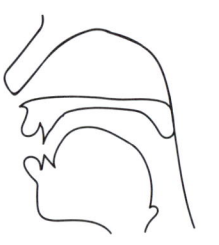

Pronunciation Tip

Compared with the lax vowel /ɪ/, the tense vowel /iy/ is pronounced with the more front part of the tongue, the tongue raised higher, the lips more spread, and the muscles more tensed. The vowel /iy/ is glided and longer, whereas the vowel /ɪ/ is not glided and is shorter. These differences make the two vowels distinct in vowel quality. Although English /iy/ and /ɪ/ differ in quality, many Korean-speaking learners of English think that the two vowels differ only in length.

PRACTICE ACTIVITIES

 LISTEN 1 (Track 9-3)

Directions

Listen and circle the odd one out. Then, check your answers.

①   a.   b.   c.
②   a.   b.   c.
③   a.   b.   c.
④   a.   b.   c.

 **LISTEN 2** (Track 9-4)

Directions

Listen and circle the word you hear. Then, check your answers.

①   Let's (fill, feel) the cup.
②   The children are drawing a (ship, sheep) together.
③   (Hit, Heat) the balloon.
④   Give me the (bin, bean).
⑤   She said, (pitch, peach).

LISTEN AND SPEAK (Track 9-5)

Directions

1. Listen and circle the word you hear. Then, check your answers. (Track 9-5-1)

   ① a. lid   b. lead
   ② a. slip   b. sleep
   ③ a. live   b. leave
   ④ a. fit   b. feet

2. Repeat the words after the speaker, paying close attention to the /iy/ and /ɪ/ sounds in the words. (Track 9-5-2)

3. Work in pairs. Partner A says one of the prompts in each pair. Partner B replies with the correct response. Once finished, switch roles.

	Prompts	Responses
①	I'm taking the (lid, lead).	a. Be careful it's hot. b. You have excellent leadership skills.
②	Did I (slip, sleep) last night?	a. You weren't hurt a lot, were you? b. Recently, you haven't slept well.
③	We'll (live, leave) downtown.	a. We enjoy the downtown hustle and bustle. b. Your friends will miss you a lot.
④	They're (fit, feet).	a. Yes, they're good looking. b. I just realized what you drew.

SPEAK 1: Tongue Twisters

> **Directions**
>
> 1. Work in pairs or small groups.
> 2. Take turns teaching English tongue twisters. One of you will be the teacher, and the rest will be students.
> 3. Once finished, switch roles.

> **Dialog**
>
> **Teacher:** Repeat these tongue twisters after me, line by line.
> *Peter cheater keeps his dinner in a tin of peas and crickets.*
>
> **Students:** *Peter cheater keeps his dinner in a tin of peas and crickets.*
>
> **Teacher:** Let's try this other one.
> *Sixty chicks, fifty sheep, are on a ship about to dip.*
> *Tim come in, quickly quick, or else the ship will surely flip.*
>
> **Students:** *Sixty chicks, fifty sheep, are on a ship about to dip.*
> *Tim come in, quickly quick, or else the ship will surely flip.*
>
> **Teacher:** Well done. Now, I'll divide the class into three teams. 1, 2, and 3, perfect. Team 1 will sing first and then team 2, and lastly, team 3. Are you ready?

SPEAK 2: OXO Game (Worksheet, pp. 221-222)

Directions

1. Work in pairs. Decide roles and choose a grid.
2. Make a sentence using one word from the row and one word from the column.
3. Flip a coin. If the coin lands on the head, you will write an X on the grid. If it lands on the tail, you will write an O on the grid. Then, write an X or O in the corresponding box after you say the sentence.
4. Keep alternating moves until one player gets OXO in a row in any direction. That player gets 1 point.
5. When the grid is filled up, the player with the most points wins.
6. You can reuse an X and/or an O even if it has been crossed out.
7. You must have a combination of OXO to win a point. No other combinations (XXX, OOO, XXO, OOX, XOX, XOO) get the point.

/ey/ as in *mate* vs. /ɛ/ as in *met*

🎧 Listen to the /ey/ and /ɛ/ sounds below. (Track 9-6)

/ey/, /ey/, /ey/, /ey/
/ɛ/, /ɛ/, /ɛ/, /ɛ/

/ey/

- Hold the front part of the tongue in the middle of the mouth, a little lower than for /ɪ/.
- As you say /ey/, raise your jaw slightly and move the front part of the tongue forward and up.
- Tense the muscles.

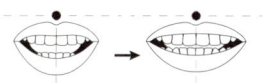
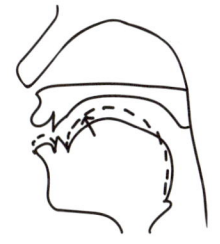

/ɛ/

- Put the front part of the tongue in the middle of the mouth, a little lower than for /ey/.
- Your tongue and the lips do not glide.
- Say /ɛ/ short.
- Relax the muscles.

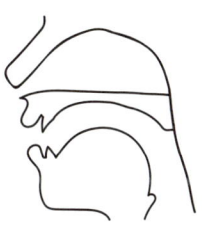

PRACTICE ACTIVITIES

 LISTEN 1 (Track 9-7)

Directions

Listen and circle the odd one out. Then, check your answers.

①   a.   b.   c.
②   a.   b.   c.
③   a.   b.   c.
④   a.   b.   c.

 LISTEN 2 (Track 9-8)

Directions

Listen and circle the word you hear. Then, check your answers.

① Let's go examine the (rake, wreck).
② The children are talking about the (pest, paste).
③ She wrote the letter in (pain, pen).
④ They (sail, sell) the boat.
⑤ She whispered, (Ed, aid).

LISTEN AND SPEAK (Track 9-9)

Directions

1. Listen and circle the word you hear. Then, check your answers. (Track 9-9-1)

①	a. debts	b. dates
②	a. west	b. waste
③	a. edge	b. age
④	a. test	b. taste

2. Repeat the words after the speaker, paying close attention to the /ey/ and /ɛ/ sounds in the words. (Track 9-9-2)
3. Work in pairs. Partner A says one of the prompts in each pair. Partner B replies with the correct response. Once finished, switch roles.

	Prompts	Responses
①	He keeps cancelling (debts, dates).	a. He's really generous. b. Perhaps, he's really busy lately.
②	It was found in the (west, waste).	a. Really, not in the east? b. It must have been thrown away.
③	We're talking about the (edge, age) of the desk.	a. It's so sharp. We need a cap for it. b. It's forty-four years old.
④	Let's (test, taste) it.	a. Sure, it works fine. b. Sure, it's delicious.

VOWELS 145

SPEAK 1: Find the Objects (Worksheet, p. 223)

Directions

1. Work in pairs.
2. In the picture, find eight objects with the sound /ey/ and eight objects with the sound /ɛ/ each. Write them on the table. Then, check your answers.

Ex. skates	Ex. desk
①	①
②	②
③	③
④	④
⑤	⑤
⑥	⑥
⑦	⑦
⑧	⑧

3. Ask and answer questions about the objects using the example conversation. Once finished, switch roles.

Example Conversation

Teacher: Now, it's time to clean up. Tidy the classroom, please.

Student: Excuse me, Miss/ Mr. _____, where can I put the *skates*?

Teacher: Put it/them *outside in the hallway*/ *in the cupboard*/ *on my desk*.

146 SOUNDS CLEAR

SPEAK 2: American Slang

> **Directions**
>
> 1. Work in pairs.
> 2. Underline the words with the sounds /ey, ɛ/ in the dialog. Then, check your answers.
> 3. Take turns saying the dialog, paying close attention to the slang words and words with the sounds /ey, ɛ/.
> 4. Once finished, switch roles.

Dialog

Stacey: Hey, bae.

Tray: Get ready.

Stacey: OK. Won't you say hi or hello? Bae, I can't decide between the red dress or the blue dress.

Tray: Stop playing games and get ready. Everybody's waiting. We're gonna be late. (*Sighs*) Women! Uh!

Stacey: Why are you acting cray? Seriously, chill out bruh! I'm taking my time because I need to slay today.

Tray: The wedding starts at 10. We have like 20 minutes to get there, and we live 40 minutes away from the venue, and you want me to chill out?

Stacey: OK, OK. I'm coming. (*Mutters to herself*) Men don't understand how hard it is to look this good.

American Slangs	Meanings
bae	an acronym for before anyone else
	a person's boyfriend or girlfriend (often used as a form of address)
cray	a short form of crazy
bruh	a male friend (often used as a form of address)
chill out	to calm down or relax
slay	greatly impress or amuse (someone)

/æ/ as in *mat* vs. /ɛ/ as in *met*

 Listen to the /æ/ and /ɛ/ sounds below. (Track 9-10)

/æ/, /æ/, /æ/, /æ/
/ɛ/, /ɛ/, /ɛ/, /ɛ/

/æ/

- Put the tongue low, dropping the jaw.
- Lips are wide open.
- Relax the muscles.

/ɛ/

- Put the front part of the tongue in the middle of the mouth, a little lower than for /ey/.
- Your tongue and lips do not glide.
- Say /ɛ/ short.
- Relax the muscles.

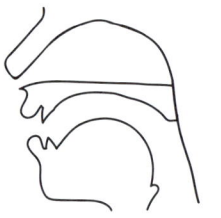

Pronunciation Tip

In English, /æ/ is produced with a more lowered tongue than /ɛ/. Although some Korean-speaking learners of English consider the English vowel /æ/ equivalent to the Korean vowel /ㅐ/ and the English vowels /ɛ/ to the Korean vowel /ㅔ/, the English vowel /æ/ is said with a more lowered tongue and relaxed muscles than /ㅐ/ and the English vowels /ɛ/ with more relaxed muscles than /ㅔ/. Moreover, in Korean, the distinction between the two vowels /ㅔ/ and /ㅐ/ has been lost. Given the influence of learners' native language on English learning, the merge of the two Korean vowels may cause difficulties for Korean-speaking learners of English to distinguish between the two English vowels /ɛ/ and /æ/ and say them accurately.

PRACTICE ACTIVITIES

 LISTEN 1 (Track 9-11)

Directions

Listen and circle the odd one out. Then, check your answers.

①   a.   b.   c.
②   a.   b.   c.
③   a.   b.   c.
④   a.   b.   c.

 LISTEN 2 (Track 9-12)

Directions

Listen and circle the word you hear. Then, check your answers.

①   We'll finally (land, lend) an airplane.
②   That (gas, guess) spreads very fast.
③   Look at the (man, men).
④   She'll (band, bend) her knees.
⑤   I whispered, (bag, beg).

LISTEN AND SPEAK (Track 9-13)

Directions

1. Listen and circle the word you hear. Then, check your answers. (Track 9-13-1)

   ① a. axe   b. x
   ② a. pan   b. pen
   ③ a. past   b. pest
   ④ a. laughed   b. left

2. Repeat the words after the speaker, paying close attention to the /æ/ and /ɛ/ sounds in each word. (Track 9-13-2)

3. Work in pairs. Partner A says one of the prompts in each pair. Partner B replies with the correct response. Once finished, switch roles.

	Prompts	Responses
①	They have a big (axe, x).	a. They'll cut the trees with it. b. They use it to express their objections.
②	I need to buy a new (pan, pen).	a. You have lots of cookware, don't you? b. You have many writing utensils, don't you?
③	We had a discussion about the (past, pest).	a. Don't make a fuss about what already happened. b. Did you find ways to prevent its spread?
④	She (laughed, left) just before you came back.	a. She's very hilarious. b. I should have arrived a little earlier.

SPEAK 1: Connect Four (Worksheet, p. 225)

Directions

1. Work in pairs.
2. Each player should choose a different color and color their box.
3. Take turns reading words aloud.
4. If you read correctly, color the word.
5. The first player with 4-in-a-row is the winner.

 SPEAK 2: A Visit to the School Nurse (Injury & Treatment Table, p. 227)

Directions

1. Work in pairs.
2. Ask and answer questions about injuries. Use the injury and treatment tables and the example conversation to help you.
3. Once finished, switch roles.

Example Conversation

School Nurse:	What's wrong?/ What's the matter?
Student:	I have _a bad cold_.
School Nurse:	Oh, that's so terrible. _Open your mouth and say ah!_/ _Do you feel pain here?_
Student:	Ah!/ Yes, I do.
School Nurse:	I'll _give you some medicine._
Student:	I really feel under the weather.
School Nurse:	Don't worry, you'll be back on your feet soon.
Student:	Thank you Ms. (or Mr.) _Mary._
School Nurse:	You're welcome. Get better soon, OK. See you later.

/ʌ/ as in *hut* vs. /ɑ/ as in *hot*

 Listen to the /ʌ/ and /ɑ/ sounds below. (Track 9-14)

/ʌ/, /ʌ/, /ʌ/, /ʌ/
/ɑ/, /ɑ/, /ɑ/, /ɑ/

/ʌ/

- Hold the tongue very neutral, dropping the jaw.
- Relax the muscles.

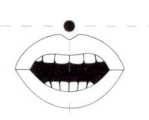
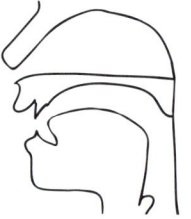

/ɑ/

- Hold the back part of the tongue, lowering it more than for any other vowel sounds.
- Drop the jaw and open the lips wide.
- Relax the muscles.

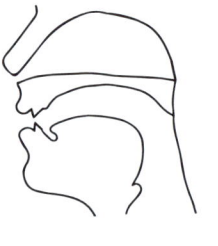

Pronunciation Tip

In English, /ʌ/ is produced with the tongue in a neutral position, whereas /ɑ/ is said with the back part of the tongue more lowered and with the mouth open wider than for /ʌ/. However, some Korean-speaking learners of English have difficulties in discriminating between these two vowel sounds.

PRACTICE ACTIVITIES

 LISTEN 1 (Track 9-15)

Directions

Listen and circle the odd one out. Then, check your answers.

① a. b. c.
② a. b. c.
③ a. b. c.
④ a. b. c.

 LISTEN 2 (Track 9-16)

Directions

Listen and circle the word you hear. Then, check your answers.

① There's a (dock, duck).
② Please, (come, calm) down and listen to him.
③ She said, (lock, luck).
④ They're hard (nuts, knots).
⑤ Its (color, collar) is white.

LISTEN AND SPEAK (Track 9-17)

Directions

1. Listen and circle the word you hear. Then, check your answers. (Track 9-17-1)

    ①   a. cut   b. cot
    ②   a. stuck   b. stock
    ③   a. cop   b. cup
    ④   a. robbed   b. rubbed

2. Repeat the words after the speaker, paying close attention to the /ʌ/ and /ɑ/ sounds in the words. (Track 9-17-2)
3. Work in pairs. Partner A says one of the prompts in each pair. Partner B replies with the correct response. Once finished, switch roles.

Prompts	Responses
① I have a (cut, cot).	a. Is it hurting?
	b. I'm trying to get my baby to sleep alone.
② They are (stuck, stock).	a. We have to have them repaired.
	b. They just arrived at the store yesterday.
③ We need a (cop, cup).	a. For an investigation.
	b. For tea.
④ Somebody (robbed, rubbed) the ring.	a. Do you mean it was stolen?
	b. That's why it's so shiny.

 SPEAK 1: Family Tree (Worksheet, pp. 229-230)

Directions

1. Work in pairs.
2. Take roles, and ask and answer questions about Logan's family members to complete his family tree.
3. Once finished, switch roles. Then, check your answers.

SPEAK 2: Common English Errors

> **Directions**
> 1. Work in pairs.
> 2. Read the two classroom scenarios and correct the mistakes. Then, check your answers.
> 3. Take roles and read the dialog out loud. Once finished, switch roles.

Scenario 1

Teacher: Today, we're going to have a funny class, and you will not be boring. But first, what did we learn on last Friday?

Student: We learned "What will you do next weekend?"

Teacher: That's right. We learned about the future tense. OK, let's quickly review by asking the question to the left person.

4 errors: _____ , _____ , _____ , _____

Scenario 2

Teacher: Look at this picture. What is it?

Student: An avocado.

Teacher: Where can I buy an avocado?

Student: At the supermarket.

Teacher: Is it a fruit or a vegetable?

Student: A fruit!

Teacher: Wonderful! Now, are you understand what means avocado?

Student: Yes.

2 errors: _____ , _____

SPEAK 3: Pronunciation Pyramid Page

> **Directions**
>
> *This activity aims for the speaker and listener to arrive at the same number on the last row.*
>
> 1. Work in pairs.
> 2. One partner reads the words until they reach the last row with numbers.
> 3. The other partner listens and follows the words. Then, they say the number the speaker stopped on.
> 4. Once finished, switch roles.

Uh - Ah

❶

Come
Color
But
Tut
Lug
Suck
What
Putt
Rut

❷

Calm
Collar
Bot
Tot
Log
Sock
Watt
Pot
Rot

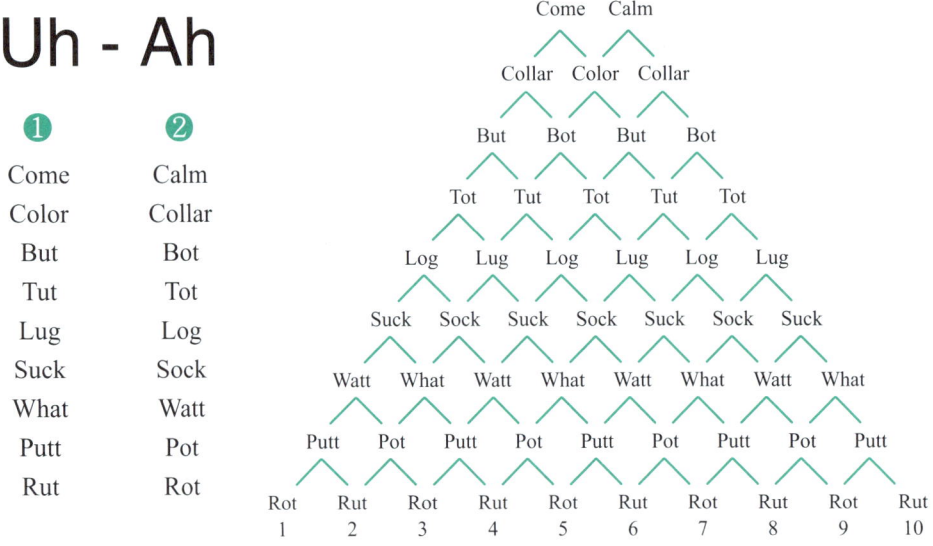

156   SOUNDS CLEAR

/uw/ as in *Luke* vs. /ʊ/ as in *look*

🎧 Listen to the /uw/ and /ʊ/ sounds below. (Track 9-18)

/uw/, /uw/, /uw/, /uw/
/ʊ/, /ʊ/, /ʊ/, /ʊ/

/uw/

- Raise the back part of the tongue high.
- Round the lips and purse them out.
- Glide the back part of the tongue upward and make the lips more round.
- Tense the muscles.

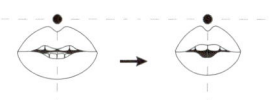 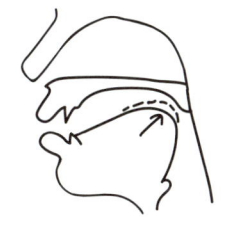

/ʊ/

- Raise the back part of the tongue high, but lower than /uw/.
- Round the lips, but less round than /uw/.
- There is no gliding of the tongue and the lips.
- Relax the muscles.

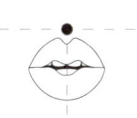 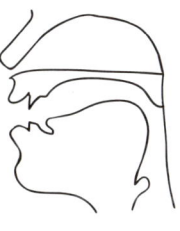

Pronunciation Tip

In comparison with the vowel /ʊ/, the vowel /uw/ is pronounced with more of the back part of the tongue, the tongue raised higher, the lips more rounded, and the muscles more tensed. In addition, the vowel /uw/ is glided and longer, whereas the vowel /ʊ/ is not glided and is shorter. English /uw/ and /ʊ/ differ in several aspects and these differences make the two vowels distinct in vowel quality. However, many Korean-speaking learners of English think that the two vowels differ only in terms of vowel length, often confusing them with one another.

PRACTICE ACTIVITIES

 LISTEN 1 (Track 9-19)

Directions

Listen and circle the odd one (vowel) out. Then, check your answers.

①   a.   b.   c.
②   a.   b.   c.
③   a.   b.   c.

 LISTEN 2 (Track 9-20)

Directions

Listen and circle the word you hear. Then, check your answers.

①   The sign says, (pool, pull).
②   How do you spell (cooed, could)?
③   This is really (full, fool) proof.
④   (Putt, Put) the balls on the grass.

LISTEN AND SPEAK (Track 9-21)

Directions

1. Listen and circle the word you hear. Then, check your answers. (Track 9-21-1)

①	a. soot	b. suit
②	a. look	b. Luke
③	a. pool	b. pull
④	a. stewed	b. stood

2. Repeat the words after the speaker, paying close attention to the /uw/ and /ʊ/ sounds in the words. (Track 9-21-2)
3. Work in pairs. Partner A says one of the prompts in each pair. Partner B replies with the correct response. Once finished, switch roles.

	Prompts	Responses
①	Clean the black (soot, suit).	a. I'll get rid of it. b. I'll take it to the dry cleaners.
②	Your (look, Luke) changes quickly.	a. She looks like a different person everyday. b. He's capricious.
③	(Pool, Pull) the toys for the children.	a. We'll donate them to an orphanage. b. They're too big for the children to move.
④	It has (stewed, stood) on the stove.	a. It's now tender. b. Move it elsewhere before you use the stove.

VOWELS 159

SPEAK 1: Blankety Blank – What to Say When…

Directions

1. The class will be divided into four teams. One person from each team will go to the front.
2. A sentence with a blank will be read out by your teacher. Each person should write down an answer.
3. If you have the same answer as your team member at the front, your team gets one point. Then, check the example answers.
4. The team with the most points wins.

Example

Teacher: You want to start the class? (Give 3 examples)

Good morning, class./ *Good* afternoon, boys and girls./ How are *you* doing?

① It's too dark.
Would you turn the lights _____? It's too dark in here.

② You need students to make space.
Could you _____ your chairs this way, please?

③ You want to explain what happens if you get the wrong answer.
You _____ a point if you answer wrong.

④ You want to compliment students. (Give 3 examples)
_____ job!/ That's quite a(n) _____!/ _____!

⑤ You want to let in more light into the room.
Can you _____ up the blinds?

⑥ A student does not know how to write the word "pudding".
How do you _____ "pudding"?

⑦ A student needs to go to the toilet.
Can I go to the _____ ?

⑧ A student wants to politely ask the teacher the meaning of a word.
_____ me, Ms. Bruce, what does "balloon" mean?

⑨ You need students to work with 4 people.
Make _____ of 4.

⑩ You want to see that all students have their books.
Hold your books _____.

⑪ You want students to bring their English books the following day.
Bring your English books _____.

⑫ It's the end of class and you will carry on the work later. We've run out of time.
We'll _____ on Tuesday.

⑬ It's time for us to work online.
Let's go to the _____ room. Wait for me before you log in.

SPEAK 2: Daily Activities (Worksheet, pp. 231-232)

Directions

1. Work in pairs.
2. Choose a worksheet, read and transcribe the activities written in phonetic symbols and write them in letters. Don't show your partner.
3. Ask your partner questions about their free time, using their timetable.
4. Write their answers in the blank, using letters.
5. Once finished, switch roles. Then, check your answers.

Example Conversation

A: Do you want to hang out with me this Monday at *5 pm*?
B: Sorry, I can't. I'm *meeting Luke*.
A: Oh, OK. How about on *Thursday* at *6 pm*?
B: I'm afraid I can't on that day, too. I'm *going to the butchers*.

/ow/ as in *no* vs. /ɔ/ as in *all* vs. /ʌ/ as in *null*

🎧 Listen to the /ow/, /ɔ/ and /ʌ/ sounds below. (Track 9-22)

/ow/, /ow/, /ow/, /ow/
/ɔ/, /ɔ/, /ɔ/, /ɔ/
/ʌ/, /ʌ/, /ʌ/, /ʌ/

/ow/

- Raise the back part of the tongue toward the roof of the mouth, but lower than /ʊ/.
- Round the lips and push them forward a bit.
- Glide the back part of the tongue upward and make the lips more round.
- Tense the muscles.

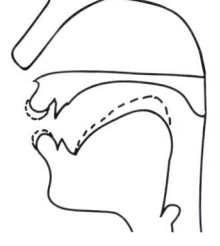

/ɔ/

- Raise the back part of the tongue toward the roof of the mouth, but lower than /ow/.
- Round the lips, but less round than /ow/.
- There is no gliding of the tongue and the lips.
- Relax the muscles.

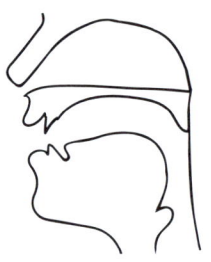

/ʌ/

- Hold the tongue very neutral, dropping the jaw.
- Relax the muscles.

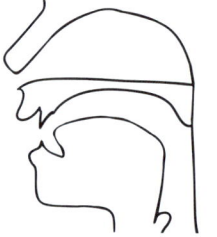

Pronunciation Tip

In comparison with the vowel /ʌ/, the vowel /ɔ/ is pronounced with the more back part of the tongue and with the lips round. However, many Korean-speaking learners of English have difficulties differentiating between the two vowels and pronouncing them accurately. In addition, they often pronounce the vowel /ow/, dropping the off-glide /w/ in the vowel, and err speaking the vowels /ow/ and /ɔ/ in words without distinction.

PRACTICE ACTIVITIES

 LISTEN 1 (Track 9-23)

Directions

Listen and circle the odd one out. Then, check your answers.

① a. b. c.
② a. b. c.
③ a. b. c.
④ a. b. c.

 LISTEN 2 (Track 9-24)

Directions

Listen and circle the word you hear. Then, check your answers.

① It was (dawn, done) when he came back.
② What does the word (low, law) mean?
③ The (cold, called) children worried their parents.
④ Did you see the sign for (dug, dog)?
⑤ He was (caught, cut) by mistake.

LISTEN AND SPEAK (Track 9-25)

Directions

1. Listen and circle the word you hear. Then, check your answers. (Track 9-25-1)

   ① a. balls   b. bowls
   ② a. lawn   b. loan
   ③ a. coughs   b. cuffs
   ④ a. boss   b. bus

2. Repeat the words after the speaker, paying close attention to the /ow/, /ɔ/, and /ʌ/ sounds in the words. (Track 9-25-2)

3. Work in pairs. Partner A says one of the prompts in each pair. Partner B replies with the correct response. Once finished, switch roles.

	Prompts	Responses
①	They bought some (balls, bowls).	a. Let's play with them. b. Wash them before putting vegetables in them.
②	The demand for that (lawn, loan) is high.	a. I also want to plant it in my garden. b. I know. Many students applied for it.
③	He always (coughs, cuffs).	a. Is he getting better? b. He is easily annoyed.
④	The (bus, boss) is coming.	a. Let's get on it. b. Let's get back to work.

SPEAK 1: Carnival Bingo (Item Table, p. 233)

Directions

Imagine you are on a school trip to the carnival.

1. Work in pairs.
2. Play rock-paper-scissors. The winner asks a question, and the loser answers. Use the item in the table and the example conversation to help you.
3. The winner crosses out the item s/he used in that question.
4. Repeat steps 2 and 3 until one of you has three bingos in any direction. The one who has three bingos first is the winner.

Example Conversation

A: What is <u>Autumn</u> doing?
B: <u>Autumn</u> is <u>on the roller coaster.</u>

 SPEAK 2: Setting Homework

Directions

Imagine you are giving homework to your class.

1. Work in pairs.
2. Take roles and read the dialog out loud.
3. Once finished, switch roles.

Dialog

Teacher: Your homework is to read the story on page 40 and do activity 4.
Student: I don't know how.
Teacher: Look at the pictures and put them in order. Look at me and I'll show you how to do it with Mr. Brown.
Student: It's too long.
Teacher: It's a short story. Stop moaning. Don't forget to take your notebooks. Well done, everyone. That's all for today.

Practice Activity Answer Keys

Chapter 1. SYLLABLE

LISTEN 1

Words	Vowel Letters	Vowel Sounds	No. of syllables
① league	4	1	1
② cheese	3	1	1
③ scrape	2	1	1
④ hormone	3	2	2
⑤ message	3	2	2
⑥ gauge	3	1	1
⑦ mystery	1	3	3

LISTEN AND SPEAK

lines	Title: An Odd Fellow Named Gus	No. of syllables
①	There was an odd fellow named Gus,	8
②	When travelling he made such a fuss,	9
③	He was banned from the train,	6
④	Not allowed on a plane,	6
⑤	And now travels only by bus.	8

LISTEN 2

① same	② same	③ different
④ different	⑤ same	⑥ same
⑦ different		

SPEAK 1

START	pencil				
	treasure				
	people	orange			
		sausage	home work	crayon	know-ledge
	teacher	palette	garbage		special
	beaker		repeat		language
	courage	August	black board	note books	challenge
					FINISH

LISTEN 3

①	2	②	2	③	2
④	1	⑤	3	⑥	1
⑦	2	⑧	2	⑨	3
⑩	4				

Chapter 2. STRESS AND UNSTRESS

PART 1: STRESS

LISTEN 1

①	a	②	b	③	b
④	a				

LISTEN 2

① same	② different	③ different
④ different	⑤ same	⑥ different
⑦ same		

LISTEN 3

①	ofFIcial	②	imMEdiate
③	ATmosphere	④	recomMEND
⑤	asSIGNment	⑥	comPEtitive
⑦	enCOUrage	⑧	maJOrity
⑨	Elegant		

PART 2: UNSTRESS

LISTEN 1

①	atom, atomic [ə] [ə]
②	rapid, rapidity [ə] [ə] [ə]
③	edit, edition [ə] [ə]
④	prefer, preference [ə] [ə][ə]
⑤	able, ability [ə][ə][ə]
⑥	botany, botanical [ə] [ə] [ə]

LISTEN 2

①	about	②	camera
③	tomorrow	④	finally
⑤	sudden	⑥	probably
⑦	different	⑧	enough
⑨	cousin		

─────── SPEAK 1 ───────

words	stress pattern	words	stress pattern
ice cream	●○	I scream	○●
selfish	●○	sell fish	○●
minute	●○	minute	○●
Korea	○●○	career	○●
history	●○○	his story	○●○
decade	●○	decayed	○●
August	●○	august	○●
pronouns	●○	pronounce	○●
Adam	●○	a dam	○●
address (n)	●○	address (v)	○●

─────── SPEAK 2 ───────

A	B
FAMily	VEGetable
BAKery	inSTEAD
aNOther	arRIVE
TAken	gaRAGE
FAVorite	CAMera

When you arRIVE at my aPARTment, you will SEE my FAVorite BAKery and a
        [ə]   [ə]   [ə]   [ə]   [ə]   [ə]   [ə]

SMALL MART that SELLS FRESH VEGetables on your LEFT. If you HAVE a
                                        [ə][ə]   [ə]   [ə]

CAR, you can PARK in the gaRAGE. If the Elevator is TAken, USE the STAIRS
  [ə]   [ə]   [ə]   [ə] [ə] [ə]   [ə]

inSTEAD. ANOther THING to MENtion is that there is a seCUrity CAMera at the
  [ə]   [ə]   [ə]   [ə] [ə]   [ə]   [ə] [ə] [ə]   [ə][ə] [ə]

ENtrance. But DON'T WORry, my FAMily will be aROUND to MEET you.
  [ə]   [ə]   [ə] [ə]   [ə]

Chapter 3. PREDICTABLE WORD STRESS

PART 1: STRESS PATTERNS ACCORDING TO SYLLABLE WEIGHT AND WORD CATEGORY

LISTEN 1

①	as**SIGN**	②	di**VORCE**
③	be**LOW**	④	**HEA**vy
⑤	**SO**fa	⑥	de**NY**
⑦	con**SIST**	⑧	cor**RECT**
⑨	e**RASE**		

LISTEN 2

①	**MO**ment	②	mu**SE**um
③	ex**PECT**	④	**PA**tient
⑤	**SO**lid	⑥	at**TEND**
⑦	**E**dit	⑧	**SI**lence
⑨	**TIC**ket		

LISTEN 3

①	a.	Did you see the (**SUS**pect)?
	b.	I (sus**PECT**) they cheated on the exam.
②	a.	Bill needs to (pro**JECT**) his voice tomorrow.
	b.	I should finish the (**PRO**ject) by tomorrow.
③	a.	I need to get a (**RE**fund) for this product.
	b.	We can't (re**FUND**) the item after the expiry date.
④	a.	They sell quality (**PRO**duces).
	b.	It (pro**DUCES**) a large amount of gas.
⑤	a.	He is going to (re**CORD**) a new song.
	b.	There is no (**RE**cord) of them in the archive.

SPEAK 2

①	Have you ever had a **CON**flict with someone?
②	Have you ever won a **CON**test?
③	Have you ever met a game **AD**dict?
④	Have you ever been someone's **SUB**ject?
⑤	Have you ever given an **IN**sult?
⑥	Have you ever tried to re**BEL**?
⑦	Have you ever been to the **DE**sert?
⑧	Have you ever taken **MI**nutes at a meeting?
⑨	Have you ever had to ad**DRESS** a large crowd?
⑩	Have you ever written a **DI**gest before?
⑪	Have you ever given a **MAN**date?
⑫	Have you ever pre**SEN**ted an assignment late?

PART 2: STRESS PATTERNS IN MORPHOLOGICALLY COMPLEX WORDS

LISTEN 1

①	disap**POINT**	②	rein**FORM**
③	misad**VISE**	④	ex-**MEM**ber
⑤	in**DOORS**	⑥	im**POS**sible
⑦	a**MO**ral	⑧	un**PLEA**sant
⑨	de**ME**rit	⑩	en**DAN**ger

LISTEN 2

①	**MEM**bership	②	**PO**werless
③	de**PEN**ding	④	**WON**derful
⑤	**TRA**veler	⑥	**NA**tural
⑦	**EA**gerly	⑧	**NEIGH**borhood
⑨	**UG**liness	⑩	**COM**fortable

LISTEN 3

①	eco**NO**mical	②	moti**VA**tion
③	ra**PI**dity	④	mys**TE**rious
⑤	per**SO**nify	⑥	co**ME**dian
⑦	e**CO**logy	⑧	engi**NEER**
⑨	employ**EE**	⑩	millio**NAIRE**
⑪	cartoo**NESQUE**	⑫	Chi**NESE**

LISTEN 4

①	**YEL**low jacket	②	**EAR**ring
③	**GREEN**house	④	**LIP**stick
⑤	ready-**MADE**	⑥	**SMOKE**-free
⑦	second**HAND**	⑧	middle-**AGED**
⑨	**HAND**write	⑩	**BA**by sit
⑪	test-**DRIVE** (verb)	⑫	double-**CLICK**

LISTEN 5

①	a.	Some students (drop **OUT**) in the middle of the semester.
	b.	The (**DROP**-out) rates were the highest last year.
②	a.	They'll (pay **BACK**) the loss as soon as they return home.
	b.	I'll use my (**PAY**back) points for this purchase.
③	a.	The new development is a remarkable (**BREAK**through).
	b.	You should (break **THROUGH**) some barriers to finish this project.
④	a.	The town has a (**BY**pass) which keeps traffic out of the center.
	b.	They (passed **BY**) the museum on the way to the park.
⑤	a.	I hope they don't (break **UP**) over this matter.
	b.	A (**BREAK**up) always hurts.
⑥	a.	She (hands **OUT**) the cakes at snack time.
	b.	There's a lady distributing (**HAND**outs) on Main Street.
⑦	a.	(Make **UP**) your mind before you leave for Chicago.
	b.	I'll have (**MAKE**up) classes next week
⑧	a.	They'll (break **DOWN**) the house from next month.
	b.	The week-by-week (**BREAK**down) helps their training.

PART 3: STRESS PATTERNS ACCORDING TO SPELLING

LISTEN 1

①	four**TEEN**		②	**SE**venty
③	him**SELF**		④	our**SELVES**
⑤	ap**PRE**ciate		⑥	**GRA**duate
⑦	re**FRI**gerate		⑧	ne**GO**tiate
⑨	**PHAR**macy		⑩	**HIS**tory

Chapter 4. Rhythm in Sentences

LISTEN 1

①	farmer/ had/ duck/ laid/ ten/ eggs	6
②	Soon/ hatched	2
③	ten/ nine/ ducklings/ looked/ mom	5
④	tenth/ one/ big/ gray/ ugly	5
⑤	other/ ducklings/ made/ fun/ ugly/ one	6
⑥	Unhappy/ farm/ poor/ duckling/ ran away/ river/ nearby	7
⑦	There/ sees/ white/ beautiful/ swans	5
⑧	Afraid/ lost/ wanted/ drown/ river	5
⑨	But/ looked/ reflection/ river	4
⑩	realized/ not/ ugly/ duckling/ but/ beautiful/ swan	7

LISTEN 2

①	can		②	can't
③	can't		④	are
⑤	weren't		⑥	shouldn't

LISTEN 3

Waitress:	Good morning. <u>Are</u> you <u>ready</u> <u>to</u> order?
Customer:	Yes, <u>for</u> <u>the</u> starter <u>I'd</u> like vegetable soup.
Waitress:	<u>And</u> what <u>would</u> <u>you</u> like <u>for</u> <u>the</u> main course?
Customer:	<u>I'd</u> like <u>a</u> T-bone steak <u>with</u> potatoes.
Waitress:	Yes, sir. How <u>would</u> <u>you</u> like <u>the</u> steak?
Customer:	Well-done, please.

Waitress:	Anything to drink?
Customer:	Yes, a cup of coffee, please.
Waitress:	Thanks.

Chapter 5. PHRASING AND LINKING

--- LISTEN 1 ---

①	You should take your car in // for service.
②	I did not know // there was milk in the refrigerator.
③	Their bike moves way faster // than your bike does.
④	Customers buy less products // whenever the price goes up.
⑤	I was snappy with him // because I was running late for work.

--- LISTEN 2 ---

①	b	②	a	③	b
④	b	⑤	a		

--- LISTEN 3 ---

①	same	②	same	③	same
④	same	⑤	same	⑥	same

--- LISTEN AND SPEAK ---

This evening // the ant told // my three-year-old daughter // that owls were nocturnal. // My daughter responded // "Yes // owls are // not turtles." //

--- SPEAK 1 ---

ToDAY was THE ABsolute WORST DAY Ever //
And DON'T TRY to conVINCE me that //
There's SOMEthing GOOD in Every DAY //
Because //, when you TAKE a CLOser LOOK // ,
This WORLD is a PREtty Evil PLACE // .
Even if
SOME GOODness does SHINE through ONCE in a WHILE //

SatisFACtion and HAPpiness DON'T LAST // .
And it's NOT TRUE that //
It's ALL in the MIND and HEART //
Because
TRUE HAPpiness CAN be atTAINED
ONly if one's surROUNdings are GOOD // .
It's NOT TRUE that GOOD Exists //
I'm SURE you can aGREE that //
The reAlity
CREATES
My ATtitude //
It's all beYOND my conTROL //
And you'll NEver in a MILlion YEARS HEAR me SAY that //
ToDAY was a VEry GOOD DAY //

--- SPEAK 2 ---

Jack and Jill	JACK and JILL went UP the HILL // to FETCH a PAIL of WAter // JACK fell DOWN and BROKE his CROWN // And JILL came TUMB-ling AFter //
Black Socks	BLACK SOCKS // they NEver get DIRty // the LONGer you WEAR them // the STRONGer they GET // someTIMES // I THINK I shad WASH them // But SOMEthing inSIDE me // SAYZ NO // NO // NOT YET //
Old Man Named Bob	ther waz an OLD MAN NAMED BOB // who Never found JOY in his JOB // he WANted to QUIT // bat he COUldn't adMIT // that he DID LOVE to HEAR himself SOB //

Chapter 6. PROMINENCE IN DISCOURSE

LISTEN 1

①	a	②	a	③	b
④	b	⑤	a	⑥	b
⑦	a	⑧	a		

LISTEN 2

He was a perPEtual MOtion maCHINE // and his MIND // was as JITtery // as his BOdy. //

The ONly TIME // I SAW LARry WORK // with CONcentrated atTENtion //

was when he MOdelled little CLAY FIGures. //

I STARTed USing PLAY dough // to FOcus his atTENtion on READing. //

We beGAN MAKing LETters and WORDS // out of PLAY dough. //

This was a TURNing point for LARry. //

He COULDN'T LEARN // at this STAGE of his LIFE // by STUDYing with PAper and PENcil. //

But he COULD LEARN // by STUDYing with BIG WADS of PLAY dough. //

SPEAK 1

I'm a STOryteller // AND // I would like to tell you a few personal stories aBOUT // what I like to call the DANger // of the single STOry // I grew up on a university CAMpus // in eastern NiGEria // my mother says that I started reading at the age of TWO // although I think four is probably close to the TRUTH // so I was an early REAder // and what I READ // were British and American children's BOOKS // I was also an early WRIter // and when I began to WRITE // at about // the age of SEven // stories in pencil with crayon illustrations that my poor mother was obligated to READ // I wrote exactly the kinds of stories I was REAding // all my characters were WHITE // and BLUE-eyed // they played in the SNOW // they ate APples // and they talked a lot about the WEAther // how lovely it was that the sun had come OUT // now this despite the FACT // that I LIVED // IN Nigeria // I had never been outSIDE Nigeria // we didn't HAVE snow // we ate MANgoes // and we never talked about the weather because there was no NEED to //

LISTEN AND SPEAK

Assistant:	May I HELP you? //
Customer:	Yes, I'd LIKE to reTURN this TOP. //
Assistant:	Can I ASK // WHY you're reTURNing THIS? //
Customer:	I BOUGHT it for my SON // but it's TOO BIG. //
Assistant:	There are NO reFUNDS // if the ITEMS were on SALE. //
Customer:	Do you HAVE the TOP // in a SMALler SIZE? //
Assistant:	Let me CHECK. //

Chapter 7. INTONATION

LISTEN 1

①	b. ↗	②	a. ↘	③	a. ↘
④	b. ↗	⑤	a. ↘	⑥	b. ↗
⑦	a. ↘	⑧	a. ↘	⑨	b. ↗
⑩	b. ↗				

LISTEN 2

①	He's late this morning ↘ // isn't he ↘ ?
②	How will you pay ↘ // cash ↗ // or card ↘ ?
③	Where are you going for your break ↘ // France ↗ // Italy ↗ // or Sweden ↗ ?
④	It's going to rain this afternoon ↘ // isn't it ↗ ?
⑤	I'm taking math ↗ // biology ↗ // calculus ↗ // and English ↘ .
⑥	What season do you like the most ↘ spring ↗ // summer ↗ // fall ↗ // or winter ↘ ?

LISTEN AND SPEAK

A:	Do you have the time ↗ ? //
B:	Yes, I do ↘ . // It's already 5:30 ↘ . //
A:	Are you coming home ↗ // or going to the office ↘ ? //
B:	I'm going to the office ↘ . //
A:	What are your plans for this weekend ↘ ? //
B:	I don't know ↘ . // Do you want to get together ↗ // or something ↗ ? //
A:	How about eating out for dinner ↘ ? //
B:	That sounds like a good idea ↘ . // Where do you want to meet ↘ ? //
A:	Let's meet at Karens' House ↘ . //
B:	Great ↘ ! // I heard they just came up with a new pizza ↗ // pasta ↗ // and dessert ↘ . //
A:	It should be good ↘ // because they always have the best food in town ↘ . //

SPEAK 1

Teacher:	Look at this **PIC**ture ↘ ! // What's different about these **BUS**ES ↘ ? // Are these buses the **SAME** ↗ ? //
Students:	**NO** ↘ . //
Teacher:	That's **RIGHT** ↘ . // These buses have **DIF**ferent colors ↘ . // Do you know '**TAYO**' ↗ ? // Let's learn colors with a fun Tayo **SONG** ↘ . // (Teacher demonstrates singing.) Let's **SING** together ↘ ! // (Sing with students) Awesome **JOB** ↘ ! //

SPEAK 2

Teacher 1:	Hello, everyone ↘ . My name is Ryan. ↘ // I'm cool, ↘ // right ↗ ? //
Teacher 2:	I'm Rachel, ↘ // and I'm kind ↘ . //
Teacher 3:	And I'm Reese. ↘ // I'm handsome. ↘ aren't I ↗ ? //
All Teachers:	We are your English teachers ↘ // today ↘ . //
Teacher 1:	(Minhee) ↗ // (What did you eat today) ↗ ? //
Student:	(Kimbap) ↘ //
Teacher 2:	That's great ↘ ! (If I want to cook that ↘ // where can I go ↘ ?) //
All Students:	(Kitchen) ↘ //
Teacher 3:	That's right ↘ . // Today's topic is ↘ // 'I'm in the kitchen' ↘ . // We are going to learn about ↘ // the names of the rooms in a house ↘ // and later we will speak with friends about it ↘ . //
All Teachers:	Are you ready ↗ ? //

174 SOUNDS CLEAR

Chapter 8. CONSONANTS

Voiceless vs. Voiced Consonants in English

LISTEN 1

①	a. pig	(b. big)
②	a. dear	(b. tear)
③	a. cold	(b. gold)
④	(a. fast)	b. vast
⑤	(a. either)	b. ether
⑥	(a. zip)	b. sip
⑦	a. cheap	(b. jeep)

/p/ as in *pin* vs. /f/ as in *fin*

LISTEN 1

①	a. pat	b. pat	(c. fat)
②	(a. leap)	b. leaf	c. leaf
③	a. fail	b. fail	(c. pail)
④	a. clip	(b. cliff)	c. clip

LISTEN 2

①	pin	②	chief	③	coughs
④	clips				

LISTEN AND SPEAK

①	a. peel	②	b. fans	③	b. cuffs
④	a. past				

/b/ as in *boat* vs. /v/ as in *vote*

LISTEN 1

①	a. vest	b. vest	(c. best)
②	(a. buy)	b. vie	c. vie
③	a. ballet	(b. valet)	c. ballet
④	a. given	b. given	(c. gibbon)

LISTEN 2

①	bowels	②	van	③	veer
④	rebel				

LISTEN AND SPEAK

①	b. veiled	②	a. base	③	a. bowed
④	b. voters				

SPEAK 2

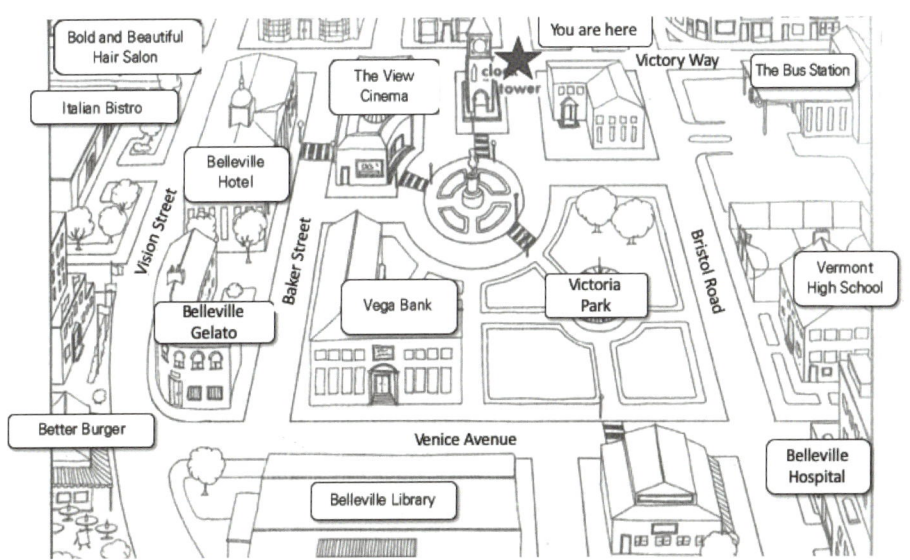

/θ/ as in *think* vs. /s/ as in *sink*

LISTEN 1

①	a. thing (circled)	b. sing	c. sing
②	a. thumb	b. thumb	c. sum (circled)
③	a. face	b. faith (circled)	c. face
④	a. pass (circled)	b. path	c. path

LISTEN 2

①	thaw	②	unsinkable
③	sums	④	thongs

LISTEN AND SPEAK

①	a. faithless	②	b. sum	③	a. mouth
④	a. tense				

/ð/ as in *though* vs. /d/ as in *dough*

LISTEN 1

Listen and circle the odd one out. Then, check your answers.

①	a. doze	b. those (circled)	c. doze
②	a. they (circled)	b. day	c. day
③	a. ladder	b. lather (circled)	c. ladder
④	a. breed (circled)	b. breathe	c. breathe

LISTEN 2

①	either	②	Dan	③	These
④	side				

LISTEN AND SPEAK

①	a. wordy	②	a. load	③	b. heather
④	b. They've				

/r/ as in *rent* vs. /l/ as in *lent*

LISTEN 1

①	a. rake (circled)	b. lake	c. lake
②	a. right	b. right	c. light (circled)
③	a. erect	b. elect (circled)	c. erect
④	a. bowl	b. bore (circled)	c. bowl

LISTEN 2

①	lock	②	readers	③	crowd
④	Kneel				

LISTEN AND SPEAK

①	a. glass	②	b. tour	③	b. prayed
④	a. flying				

/ʒ/ as in *usual* vs. /dʒ/ as in *judge*, /z/ as in *zoo*

LISTEN 1

①	a. ledger	b. leisure (circled)	c. ledger
②	a. bays	b. bays	c. beige (circled)
③	a. jute (circled)	b. zoot	c. zoot
④	a. cage	b. cage	c. Ks (circled)

LISTEN 2

①	pledger	②	rouge	③	Zach
④	fridge				

LISTEN AND SPEAK

①	a. legion	②	a. closure	③	b. rays
④	b. zoos				

Chapter 9. VOWELS

/iy/ as in *leap* vs. /ɪ/ as in *lip*

LISTEN 1

①	a. peak	b. peak	**c. pick**
②	a. pill	**b. peel**	c. pill
③	a. beat	b. beat	**c. bit**
④	**a. green**	b. grin	c. grin

LISTEN 2

①	feel	②	ship	③	Hit
④	bean	⑤	pitch		

LISTEN AND SPEAK

①	a. lid	②	b. sleep	③	b. leave
④	a. fit				

SPEAK 1

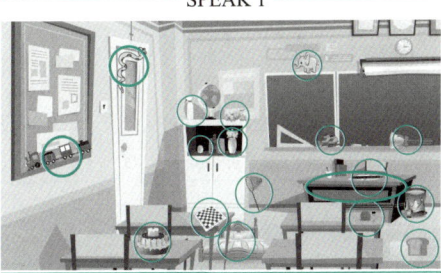

/ey/	/ɛ/
1. snake	1. pen
2. train	2. egg
3. grapes	3. elephant
4. vase	4. bed
5. cake	5. bread
6. paint	6. net
7. spray	7. chess
8. snail	8. bell

SPEAK 2

words with /ey/	hey, bae, OK, say, playing, games, waiting, late, cray, taking, slay, today, away
words with /ɛ/	get, ready, red, dress, everybody, wedding, get, venue

/ey/ as in *mate* vs. /ɛ/ as in *met*

LISTEN 1

①	**a. gate**	b. get	c. get
②	a. mate	**b. met**	c. mate
③	a. fail	**b. fell**	c. fail
④	a. bet	b. bet	**c. bate**

LISTEN 2

①	rake	②	pest	③	pen
④	sail	⑤	aid		

LISTEN AND SPEAK

①	a. debts	②	a. west	③	b. age
④	a. test				

/æ/ as in *mat* vs. /ɛ/ as in *met*

LISTEN 1

①	a. mat	**b. met**	c. mat
②	**a. wreck**	b. rack	c. rack
③	a. Ed	**b. add**	c. Ed
④	a. pet	b. pet	**c. pat**

LISTEN 2

①	land	②	guess	③	men
④	band	⑤	bag		

LISTEN AND SPEAK

①	b. X	②	a. pan	③	a. past
④	b. left				

/ʌ/ as in *hut*, /ɑ/ as in *hot*

LISTEN 1

①	a. hot	**b. hut**	c. hot
②	**a. bot**	b. but	c. but
③	a. fond	b. fond	**c. fund**
④	**a. sock**	b. suck	c. suck

LISTEN 2

①	duck	②	calm	③	lock
④	nuts	⑤	collar		

LISTEN AND SPEAK

①	b. cot	②	a. stuck	③	b. cup
④	a. robbed				

SPEAK 1

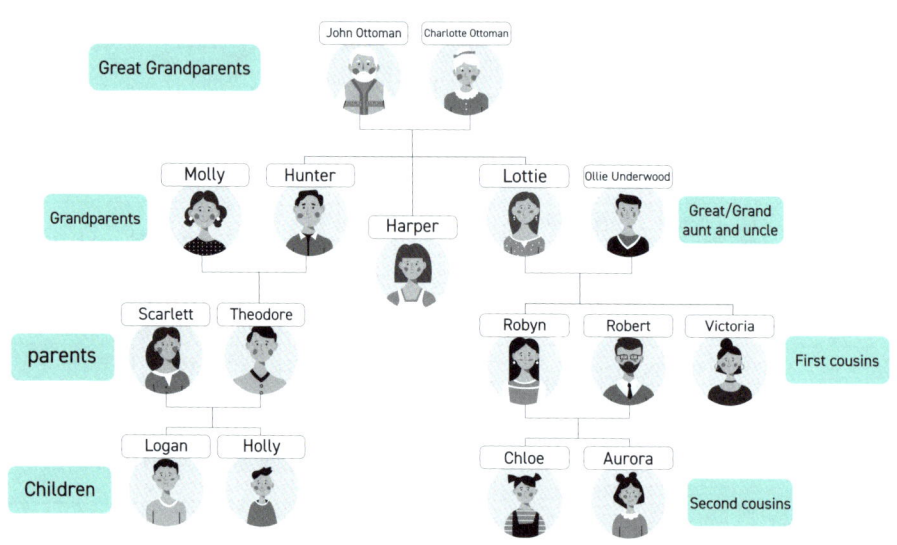

SPEAK 2

Scenario 1	
Teacher:	Today we are going to have a <u>fun</u> class and you will not be <u>bored</u>. But first, what did we learn <u>last Friday</u>?
Teacher:	That's right. We learned about the future tense. OK, let's quickly review by asking the question <u>to the person on the left</u>.

Scenario 2	
Teacher:	Wonderful! Now, <u>do</u> you understand what <u>avocado means</u>?

/uw/ as in *Luke* vs. /ʊ/ as in *look*

LISTEN 1

①	a. foot	b. loot	c. moot
②	a. mook	b. cook	c. duke
③	a. good	b. food	c. would

(circled: a. foot, c. duke, b. food)

LISTEN 2

①	pull	②	cooed	③	fool
④	Putt				

LISTEN AND SPEAK

①	b. suit	②	a. look	③	a. pool
④	b. stood				

SPEAK 1

①	Would you turn the lights **on**?
②	Could you **move** your chairs this way, please?
③	You **lose** a point if you answer wrong.
④	**Good** job!/That's quite an **improvement**!/ **Superb**!
⑤	Can you **pull** up the blinds?
⑥	How do you **spell** "pudding"?
⑦	Can I go to the **restroom**?
⑧	**Excuse** me, Ms. Bruce what does "balloon" mean?
⑨	Make **groups** of 4.
⑩	Hold your books **up**.
⑪	Bring your English books **tomorrow**.
⑫	We've run out of time. We'll **continue** on Tuesday.
⑬	Let's go to the **computer** room. Wait for me before you log in.

178 SOUNDS CLEAR

SPEAK 2

WORKSHEET (A)

Your Partner's Timetable

	Monday	Tuesday	Thursday	Sunday
5 pm	meeting Luke	foot massage	cooking class	meeting my crew
6 pm	food shopping	making a fool	going to the butcher	watching the moon
9 pm	buy sugar	photo shoot	wash pet wolf	picking mushrooms

WORKSHEET (B)

Your Partner's Timetable

	Monday	Wednesday	Saturday	Sunday
3 pm	cleaning bedroom	making soup	going to school	watching flowers bloom
7 pm	getting some wool	cooking stewed chicken	buying some bullets	washing cushions
8 pm	fixing fishing hook	getting a flu jab	brewing beer	eating pudding

/ow/ as in *no*, vs. /ɔ/ as in *all* vs. /ʌ/ as in *null*

LISTEN 1

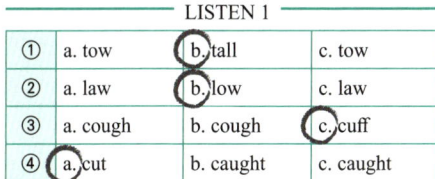

①	a. tow	b. tall	c. tow
②	a. law	b. low	c. law
③	a. cough	b. cough	c. cuff
④	a. cut	b. caught	c. caught

LISTEN 2

| ① | dawn | ② | low | ③ | cold |
| ④ | dug | ⑤ | caught | | |

LISTEN AND SPEAK

| ① | a. balls | ② | b. loan | ③ | a. coughs |
| ④ | a. boss | | | | |

APPENDIX
Activity Worksheet

Chapter 1 – SPEAK 1: Syllable Maze

WORKSHEET

Start	pencil	clip	highlighter	dictionary	binder	funnel
exercise	treasure	protractor	library	tape	compass	beautiful
theater	people	orange	globe	eraser	terrible	stapler
banana	chalk	sausage	kangaroo	homework	crayon	knowledge
calculator	teacher	palette	opinion	garbage	guide	special
ballpoint	beaker	sharpener	pins	repeat	interest	language
calendar	courage	August	blackboard	notebooks	xylophone	challenge
ruler	happiness	birthday	afternoon	illustrate	excellent	Finish

Chapter 2 – SPEAK 1: Word Stress Bingo

WORKSHEET

Chapter 3 – PART 1 – SPEAK 2: Have You Ever…?

Word Bank

desert, digest, conflict, address, addict, contest, insult, subject, minutes, mandate, rebel, presented

WORKSHEET

Have you ever had a _____ with someone? Name:	Have you ever won a _____? Name:	Have you ever met a game _____? Name:
Have you ever been someone's _____? Name:	Have you ever given an _____? Name:	Have you ever tried to _____? Name:
Have you ever been to the _____? Name:	Have you ever taken _____ at a meeting? Name:	Have you ever had to _____ a large crowd? Name:
Have you ever written a _____ before? Name:	Have you ever given a _____? Name:	Have you ever _____ an assignment late? Name:

Chapter 3 – PART 2 – SPEAK 1: College Life Dice Bingo

WORKSHEET

Roll the Dice	⚀	⚁	⚂	⚃	⚄	⚅
⚀	Is it hard to get into a relationship at college?	Do freshmen have to take biology?	Do you volunteer?	Do you watch a lot of tutorials?	Are you a procrastinator?	Was it easy to get admission into college?
⚁	What's your major?	When will you graduate?	What are 5 essential items students need?	Is college life chaotic?	What is unique about you?	Did you study Chinese in high school?
⚂	What do you do on weekends?	Do you live in the dormitory, a private house or at home?	What were you like at 15?	What would you say to your 90-year-old self?	Do you have to attend all classes?	What is your most unforgettable moment at college?
⚃	Are you glad you don't have to wear a uniform?	If your friends are fighting, would you intervene?	What's your biggest achievement?	Are you a fearless or fearful person?	Is appearance important to you?	What clubs are you involved in?
⚄	Tell me about a time you had to be courageous.	What is your favorite spot on campus?	What's your favorite cafeteria dish?	Do you think girls and boys can be friends?	What can you do if you don't like your roommate(s)?	Is there anything you like doing by yourself?
⚅	Do you enjoy doing group projects?	Do you have your driver's permit?	What are some disadvantages of college life?	How often do you work out?	What's the best excuse you've heard someone say for missing a class?	What celebrations/festivals do you enjoy most?

Chapter 3 – PART 2 – SPEAK 2: The Perfect Date Survey

WORKSHEET

Interviewee	Me	1)	2)	3)	4)
Your perfect date should be at: A mysterious location A picturesque location A luxurious restaurant An unconventional location					
Your perfect date includes: Stimulating conversations A unique moment A gorgeous view of the Han River Delicious food					
The first thing you notice on a date is: Personality Likeability Financial capabilities Communication is static					
Your favorite part of a relationship is: Traveling together Volunteering Having a strong intellectual connection Becoming official					
Ideal holiday destination together: A romantic European getaway A thrilling tour of an undiscovered country Exotic beaches – unadventurous but relaxing A rustic cabin in the woods					
You know you're in love when: You smile hideously when his/her name is mentioned You procrastinate your work You communicate together constantly You coordinate outfits accidentally					

Chapter 3 – PART 3 – SPEAK 1: Ty & Teen Snakes and Ladders

WORKSHEET

Finish	r 64-48	q 60-42	p 42-28
l 35-16	m 30-17	n 41+19	o 80-64
k 72+18	j 53-13	i 57+17	h 26-13
d 30-13	e 40-26	f 50-30	g 15+15
c 55+15	b 34+16	a 90-75	Start

Chapter 4 – SPEAK 2: Team Project

WORKSHEET

Timetable for Student 1

Time	Monday	Tuesday	Friday	Saturday
9:00 am	English Writing		English Conversation	Dentist Appointment
10:00 am		English Conversation		
11:00 am			History	
12:00 pm	Lunch Cafeteria	Lunch Kimbap World	Lunch Cafeteria	Lunch with Mom
1:00 pm	Science			
2:00 pm	Math	P.E.		Movie

APPENDIX: Activity Worksheet

Chapter 4 – SPEAK 2: Team Project

WORKSHEET

Timetable for Student 2

Time	Monday	Tuesday	Friday	Saturday
9:00 am				Tennis
10:00 am		Computing	English Conversation	
11:00 am	Career Advice			Hair Appointment
12:00 pm	Lunch Chez Kim	Lunch The Best Burger	Lunch Cafeteria	Lunch Home
1:00 pm		Geography	Pilates Class	
2:00 pm	P.E.			Homework Café Gusto

196 SOUNDS CLEAR

Chapter 4 – SPEAK 2: Team Project

WORKSHEET

Timetable for Student 3

Time	Monday	Tuesday	Friday	Saturday
9:00 am			English Conversation	Tutoring English
10:00 am			English Conversation	
11:00 am	P.E.		P.E.	
12:00 pm	Lunch Cafeteria	Lunch Kimbap World	Lunch Cafeteria	Lunch Home
1:00 pm		History		
2:00 pm	English Writing	History	Yoga Class	Meeting Friends Cafe Gusto

Chapter 4 – SPEAK 2: Team Project

Timetable for Student 4

Time	Monday	Tuesday	Friday	Saturday
9:00 am				
10:00 am		Computing	English Conversation	
11:00 am				
12:00 pm	Lunch Cafeteria	Lunch Lava Llama	Lunch Cafeteria	Lunch Cafeteria
1:00 pm	Art	Animation		
2:00 pm			Tutoring Math	Soccer

WORKSHEET

Chapter 6 – SPEAK 2: Focus Tic Tac Toe

WORKSHEET (A)

In my opinion _____ are the best band in the world.	In **my** opinion _____ are the best band in the world.	In my **opinion** _____ are the best band in the world.
In my opinion _____ are the best band **in** the world.	In my opinion _____ are the best band in the **world**.	In my opinion _____ are **the** best band in the world.
In my opinion _____ are the **best** band in the world.	In my opinion _____ are the best **band** in the world.	In my opinion _____ are the best band in **the** world.

I didn't say he stole the money.	I **didn't** say he stole the money.	I didn't **say** he stole the money.
I didn't say **he** stole the money.	I didn't say he stole the **money**.	I didn't say he **stole** the money.
I didn't say he stole **the** money.	I didn't say he stole the money, **did** I?	I didn't say he stole the money, did **I**?

APPENDIX: Activity Worksheet

Chapter 6 – SPEAK 2: Focus Tic Tac Toe

WORKSHEET (B)

Mom I said I passed the test yesterday.	Mom **I** said I passed the test yesterday.	Mom I **said** I passed the test yesterday.
Mom I said **I** passed the test yesterday.	Mom I said I passed the test **yesterday**.	Mom I said I **passed** the test yesterday.
Mom I said I passed the **test** yesterday.	Mom I **didn't** say I passed the test yesterday.	Mom I said I **didn't** pass the test yesterday.

John used to work for the newspaper that you are reading.	John **used** to work for the newspaper that you are reading.	John used to **work** for the newspaper that you are reading.
John used to work for the **newspaper** that you are reading.	John used to work for the newspaper that you are **reading**.	John used to work for the newspaper that **you** are reading.
John used to work for the newspaper that you **are** reading.	John used to **read** the newspaper that you are reading.	John **never** used to work for the newspaper that you are reading.

Chapter 7 – SPEAK 3: Intonation Bingo

WORKSHEET

Emotion Table

Roll the Dice	⚀	⚁	⚂	⚃	⚄	⚅
⚀ / ⚁	sarcastic		happy		afraid	
⚂ / ⚃	angry		surprised		annoyed	
⚄ / ⚅	sad		disbelief		shy	

APPENDIX: Activity Worksheet

Chapter 7 – SPEAK 3: Intonation Bingo

WORKSHEET

Intonation Bingo

I have a stomachache.	Be quiet!	Can I go to the bathroom?	I'm hungry.
I'm sorry, I don't understand.	Could you repeat the instructions, please?	Is this a pencil, a pen or a marker?	It's hard, I don't know the answer sir.
I forgot to bring my homework.	I didn't bring my English book.	Work in pairs.	You need glue, scissors, an eraser and…?
Can you help me, please?	Teacher, I can have one more Choco-pie, can't I?	Will class finish early today?	Take one sheet and pass them on.

Chapter 7 — SPEAK 4: The Finish Line

WORKSHEET

⚀	⚁	⚂	⚃	⚄	⚅
You know what I mean.	The Taj Mahal is in India, right?	They said no.	Eyes to the front.	Make groups of 4?	Will you marry me or him?
Would you like coffee, tea, or water?	Sit down!	Do you like this shirt?	I hope you have a nice weekend.	Come here right now?	Do you enjoy reading, cooking, biking, running…?
Hurry up!	Where did you go?	What's the best city to live in Chuncheon, Seoul, Busan…?	I'm sorry I'm late.	Excuse me, Ms. Kim, is this all right?	They said no?
What's your favorite color?	Sit down.	You know what I mean?	How do you spell "orange"?	I'm sorry I'm late?	See you tomorrow?
Come here right now!	You're going to meet me in Hongdae, aren't you?	Make groups of 4.	Chicken is much better than pizza, isn't it?	Me?	Is anyone having trouble?
Me.	Give that back!	Houses in Seoul are very expensive, aren't they?	See you tomorrow.	Which movie do you want to see?	New Zealand is really beautiful, isn't it?
FINISH	FINISH	FINISH	FINISH	FINISH	FINISH

Chapter 8 – /p/ vs. /f/ – SPEAK 2: Are You Adulting?

WORSHEET

	You	Friend 1	Friend 2
1. You live in private accommodation.			
2. You often watch frugal living videos.			
3. You separate your trash regularly.			
4. You forgot when you last partied.			
5. A perfect Friday night is staying at home and watching films.			
6. You are asleep before midnight.			
7. You collect coupons.			
8. You pay your own phone bill.			
9. You frequently do your laundry.			
10. You attempt to make a list before going shopping.			
11. You compare food prices and buy the cheapest deal.			
12. You take vitamin pills.			
13. You clean up frequently.			
14. You prefer cooking fresh meals instead of splashing out on a takeout.			
15. You pay for friends when eating out.			
16. You use a financial planner to track your spending.			
17. You follow a strict morning routine (e.g., working out, eating breakfast, etc.).			
18. You favour making coffee at home instead of buying one from the coffee shop.			
19. If something is too expensive, you don't ask your parents for it. Instead, you save up to buy it.			
20. It is your opinion that people who wake up in the afternoon on weekends are lazy.			
Total			

Chapter 8 – /b/ vs. /v/ – SPEAK 1: Guess Who

Character Bank

Clive	Elvis	Benji	Olivia	Eva
Abigale	Beverley	Kevin	Devonte	Davina
Evelyne	Harve	Victoria	Trevor	Hubert
Naveka	Giovani	Vanessa	Bert	Vivienne
Veronica	Xavier	Vava	Victory	Baxter

APPENDIX: Activity Worksheet

WORKSHEET (A)

Chapter 8 – /b/ vs. /v/ – SPEAK 2: Giving Directions

Italian Bistro, Belleville Hotel, Better Burger, Vermont High School, Vega Bank

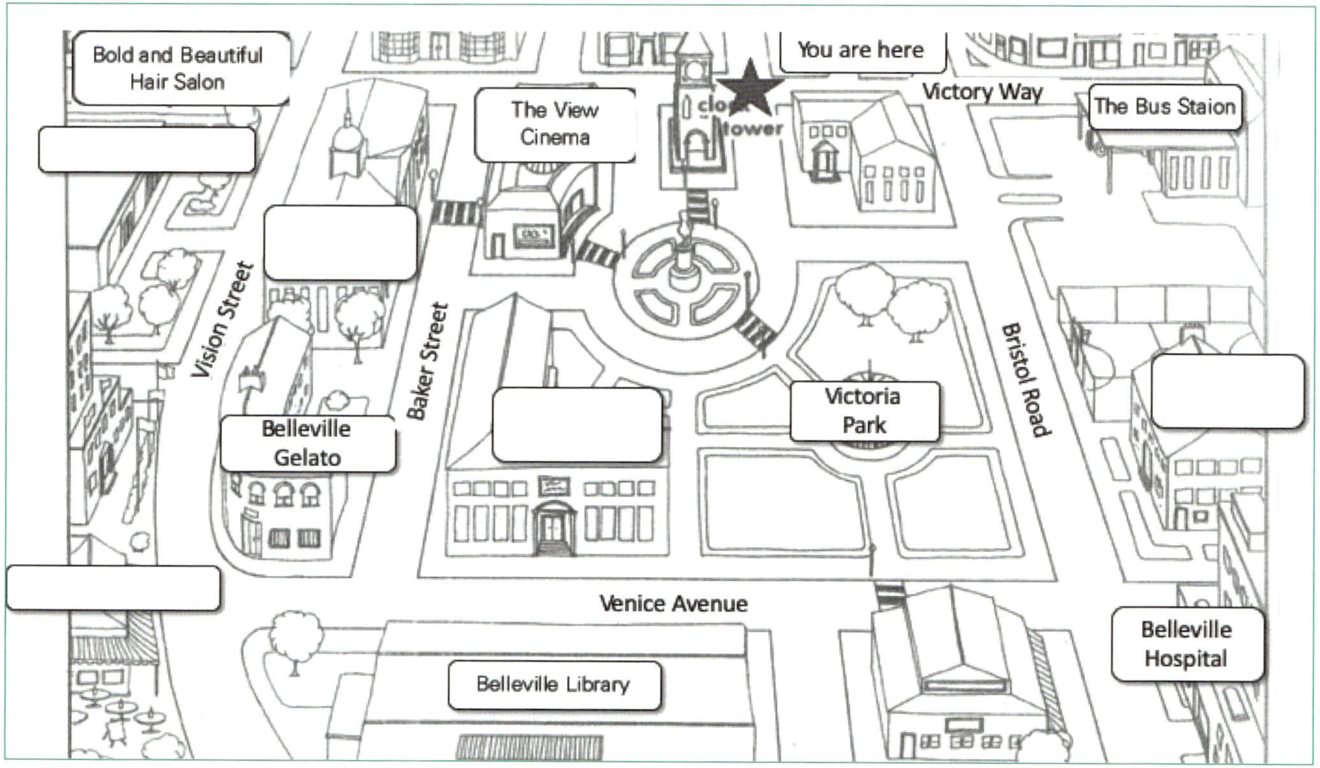

APPENDIX: Activity Worksheet

Chapter 8 – /b/ vs. /v/ – SPEAK 2: Giving Directions

The View Cinema, Belleville Gelato, The Bus Station, Bold and Beautiful Hair Salon, Belleville Hospital

WORKSHEET (B)

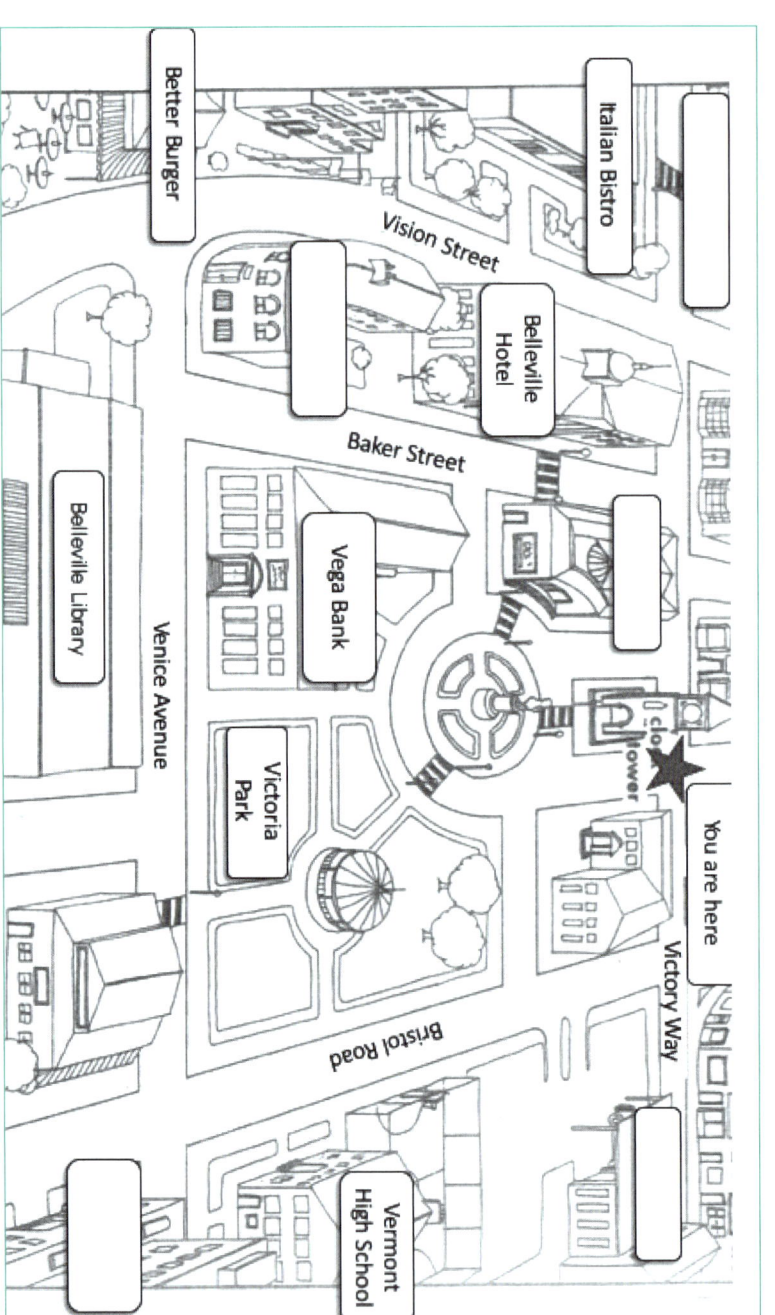

210 SOUNDS CLEAR

Chapter 8 – /θ/ vs. /s/ – **SPEAK 2: Battleship**

Round 1

My Ships

	Tuesday	Wednesday	Thursday	Saturday	Sunday
Sleet					
Blustery					
Snowy					
Thunder					
Thaw					
Ice storm					

My Enemy's Ships

	Tuesday	Wednesday	Thursday	Saturday	Sunday
Sleet					
Blustery					
Snowy					
Thunder					
Thaw					
Ice storm					

Chapter 8 – /θ/ vs. /s/ – SPEAK 2: Battleship

Round 2

My Ships

	Tuesday	Wednesday	Thursday	Saturday	Sunday
Misty					
Blizzard					
-13					
Frosty					
Thermal					
Thunderstorm					

My Enemy's Ships

	Tuesday	Wednesday	Thursday	Saturday	Sunday
Misty					
Blizzard					
-13					
Frosty					
Thermal					
Thunderstorm					

Chapter 8 – /ð/ vs. /d/ – SPEAK 1: Whose Is It?

WORKSHEET

START

clothes/ these **Heather** →	video game/ this **Edith** ↑	bathing suits/ these **Andrew** ↑
leather jacket/ that **Dorcas**	doughnuts/ those **Ruther** ↓	smoothies/ those **Jessie** ↓
wood lathes/ these **Mordechai** →	Father's Day card/ this **Devon** ↑	feather bowers/ those **Dominic** ↑
	shaving lather/ that **Jonathan** ↑	teething toys/ those **Alden** ↑
		a wedding ring/ this **Dasha**

FINISH

APPENDIX: Activity Worksheet

Chapter 8 – /ð/ vs. /d/ – SPEAK 2: Desert Island

Item Box			
a bathing suit	a fishing rod	a diary	a tetherball
a calendar	a leather jacket	a smoothie maker	a first aid kit
a hand saw	soothing gel	bathing soap	a dog
a clothing line	knee pads	a head band	dates
a radio	a feather pen	a screwdriver	cards

① _____

② _____

③ _____

Chapter 8 – /r/ vs. /l/ – **SPEAK 1: The Dial Pad Game**

WORKSHEET

Dial Pad 1

0 really	1 rally	2 light	3 right	4 alive
5 arrive	6 collect	7 correct	8 lentil	9 rental

Chapter 8 – /r/ vs. /l/ – SPEAK 1: The Dial Pad Game

Dial Pad 2

WORKSHEET

0 loyal	1 royal	2 play	3 flea	4 blacken
5 lime	6 pray	7 free	8 rhyme	9 bracken

218 SOUNDS CLEAR

Chapter 8 – /ʒ/ vs. /dʒ/ vs. /z/ – SPEAK 1: Dots and Boxes

WORKSHEET

visual	illusion	Georgia	leisure	exposure	
amnesia	educate	reject	Egypt	Roger	
usually	judge	profusion	dozen	booze	
soldier	zero	generation	conclusion	cozy	
treasure	Nigeria	citizen	Belgium	rouge	
magazine	clothes	seclusion	husband	cordial	
huge	message	freeze	gender	genre	
pleasure	executive	gypsy	Missouri	Zaire	

Chapter 9 – /iy/ vs. /ɪ/ – **SPEAK 2: OXO Game**

WORKSHEET (Grid 1)

	cheese	bleed	peach
like			
guess			
lesson			

Chapter 9 – /iy/ vs. /ɪ/ – SPEAK 2: OXO Game

WORKSHEET (Grid 2)

	light	sit	review
keep			
let's			
first			

222　SOUNDS CLEAR

WORKSHEET

Chapter 9 – /ey/ vs. /ɛ/ – SPEAK 1: Find the Objects

Chapter 9 – /æ/ vs. /ɛ/ – SPEAK 1: Connect Four

WORKSHEET

Player 1: Color box	Player 2: Color box

X	AXE	PEN	PAN	MEN	MAN	MAT
MET	GEM	JAM	BREAD	BRAD	SET	SAT
TEN	TAN	PEP	PAP	BET	BAT	TREK
TRACK	GUESS	GAS	HEAD	HAD	PENNY	ANNIE
RENT	RANT	END	AND	LEST	LAST	PECK
PACK	SEND	SAND	HEM	HAM	PET	PAT

Chapter 9 – /æ/ vs. /ɛ/ – SPEAK 2: A Visit to the School Nurse

WORKSHEET

Injury

a bruised elbow	a black eye	chicken pox	a rash on my left hand	a leg cramp	a splitting headache
a sprained ankle	a backache	asthma and my chest hurts	an allergy	swelling on my neck	a bad cold

Treatment

Put you on bed rest.	Give you a bandage.	Put a cast on.
Give you some medicine.	Call the ambulance.	Take your temperature.
Give you an eye exam.	Give you some vitamin tablets.	Give you some aloe vera gel.

APPENDIX: Activity Worksheet

Chapter 9 – /ʌ/ vs. /ɑ/ – SPEAK 1: Family Tree

WORKSHEET (A)

Partner A

Logan's Missing Family Members	Answers for B
1. Who's John?	Charlotte is Logan's great grandmother.
2. Who's Theodore?	Robyn is Logan's first cousin.
3. Who's Lottie?	Harper is Logan's great/grand aunt.
4. Who's Victoria?	Molly is Logan's grandmother.
5. Who's Aurora?	Scarlett is Logan's mother.

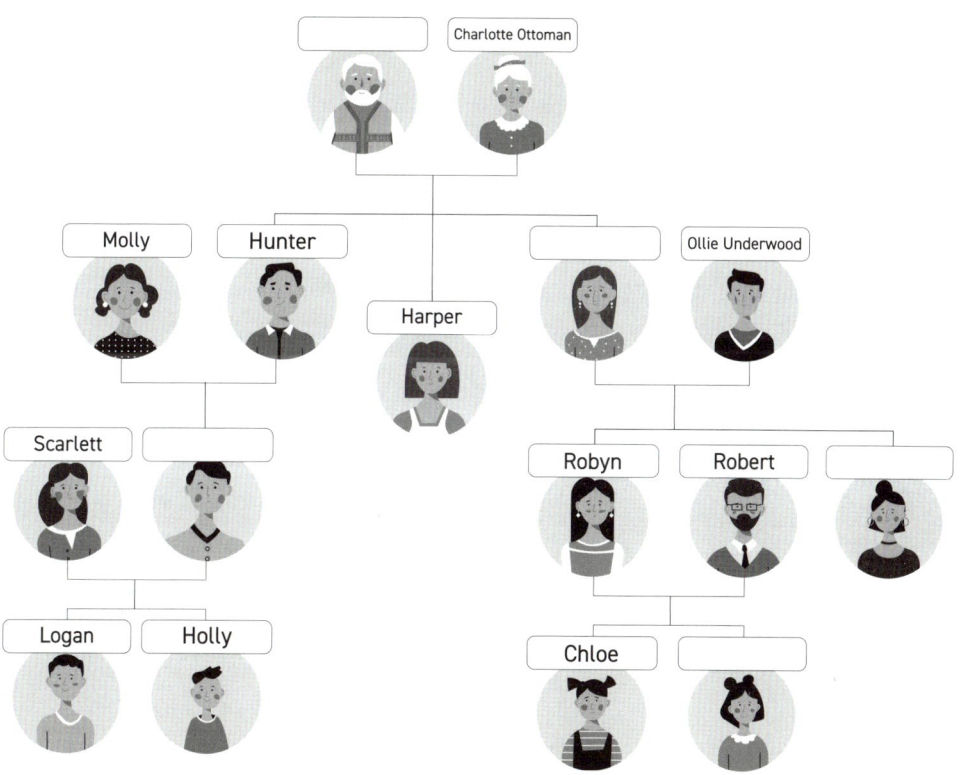

APPENDIX: Activity Worksheet

Chapter 9 – /ʌ/ vs. /ɑ/ – SPEAK 1: Family Tree

WORKSHEET (B)

Partner B

Logan's Missing Family Members	Answers for A
1. Who's Charlotte?	John is Logan's great grandfather.
2. Who's Robyn?	Theodore is Logan's father.
3. Who's Harper?	Lottie is Logan's great/grand aunt.
4. Who's Molly?	Victoria is Logan's first cousin.
5. Who's Scarlett?	Aurora is Logan's second cousin.

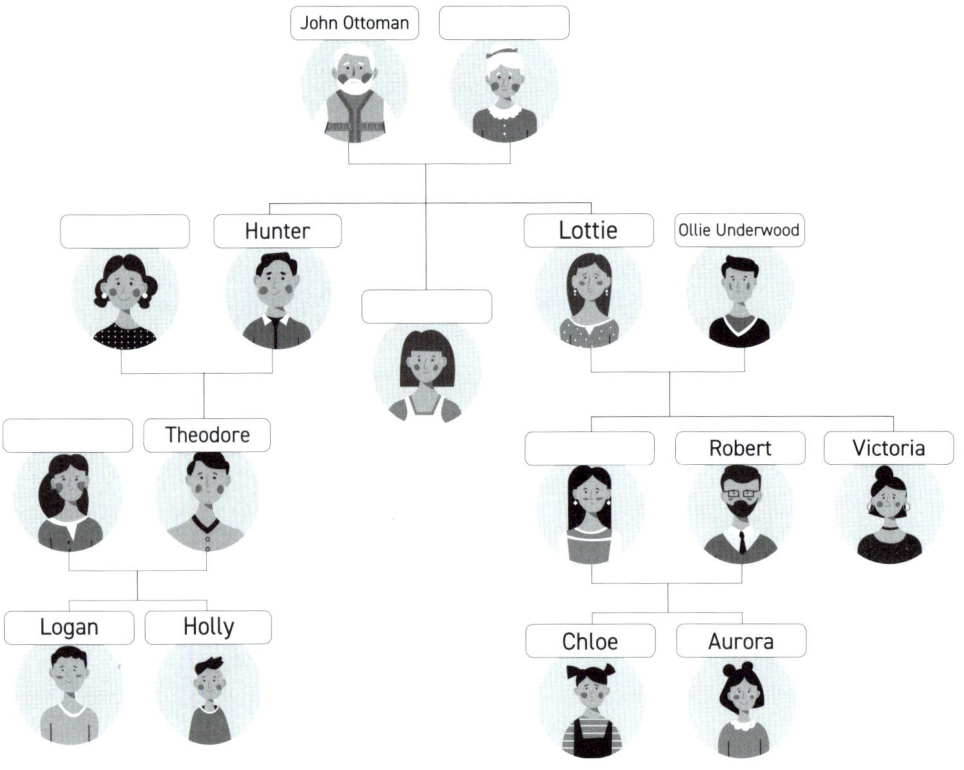

230   SOUNDS CLEAR

Chapter 9 – /uw/ vs. /ʊ/ – SPEAK 2: Daily Activities

WORKSHEET (A)

Your Timetable

	Monday	Wednesday	Saturday	Sunday
3 pm	/ˈkliynɪŋ ˈbɛdˌruwm/ ( )	/ˈmeykɪŋ suwp/ ( )	/ˈgowɪŋ tə skuwl/ ( )	/ˈwɑtʃɪŋ ˈflawəz bluwm/ ( )
7 pm	/ˈgɛtɪŋ sʌm wʊl/ ( )	/ˈkʊkɪŋ styuwd ˈtʃɪkɪn/ ( )	/ˈbayɪŋ sʌm ˈbʊləts/ ( )	/ˈwɑʃɪŋ ˈkʊʃənz/ ( )
8 pm	/ˈfɪksɪŋ ˈfɪʃɪŋ hʊk/ ( )	/ˈgɛtɪŋ ə fluw dʒæb/ ( )	/ˈbruwɪŋ bɪər/ ( )	/ˈiytɪŋ ˈpʊdɪŋ/ ( )

Your Partner's Timetable

	Monday	Tuesday	Thursday	Sunday
5 pm	meeting Luke			
6 pm				
9 pm				

APPENDIX: Activity Worksheet

Chapter 9 – /uw/ vs. /ʊ/ – SPEAK 2: Daily Activities

WORKSHEET (B)

Your Timetable

	Monday	Tuesday	Thursday	Sunday
5 pm	/ˈmiytɪŋ luwk/ ( )	/fʊt məˈsɑʒ/ ( )	/ˈkʊkɪŋ klæs/ ( )	/ˈmiytɪŋ may kruw/ ( )
6 pm	/fuwd ˈʃɑpɪŋ/ ( )	/ˈmeykɪŋ ə fuwl/ ( )	/ˈgowɪŋ tə ðə ˈbʊtʃər/ ( )	/ˈwɑtʃɪŋ ðə muwn/ ( )
9 pm	/bay ˈʃʊgər/ ( )	/ˈfowtə ʃuwt/ ( )	/waʃ pɛt wʊlf/ ( )	/ˈpɪkɪŋ ˈmʌʃrʊmz/ ( )

Your Partner's Timetable

	Monday	Wednesday	Saturday	Sunday
3 pm	cleaning bedroom			
7 pm				
8 pm				

Chapter 9 – /ow/ vs. /ɔ/ vs. /ʌ/ – SPEAK 1: Carnival Bingo

Item Table

 **Otis** drinking soda	 **Paula** stroking a pony	 **Milo** playing on a game console	 **Audrey** buying a gift at the gift store
 **Willow** riding on a go-kart	 **Eloise** watching a circus show	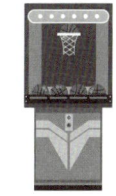 **Holden** playing at the basketball stall	 **Leo** waiting to ride the freefall tower
 **Royalty** standing at the fishbowl stall	 **Rowen** on the merry-go-round	 **Joyce** on the swinging boat	 **Noah** playing at the toy stall
 **Autumn** on the roller coaster	 **Nora** won a goldfish	 **Zoe** getting some gumball	 **Aurora** playing the Whac-A-Mole game